Praise for *Writing with Grace*

"This is a beautiful book about a very human story. In learning to embrace the Real Truth in the other, we learn to embrace our own Real Truth. With simple honesty, Grace and Judy have shared the Real Truth of their journey together. And if we accept it, we are challenged to make that journey our own."

—Jean Vanier, author of *Becoming Human*, founder of L'Arche

"When Judy McFarlane met Grace Chen, she discovered a young writer with the fierce desire for creative expression she felt in herself. What transpired was a gift to both of them. Informative, absorbing, and moving, *Writing with Grace* is a delight."

—Joan Thomas, author of *Curiosity*

"There is as much thinking as feeling in and that's what make it so exceptional. at every level. One of the many deep Farlane poses is: who is more enlighten. This book is the antidote to a culture that promotes success at all costs without ever asking what success is."

—Ian Brown, author of *The Boy in the Moon:
A Father's Search for his Disabled Son*

"McFarlane's writing is accomplished, intimate and brimming with insight that inspires us to re-examine our attitudes towards both ourselves and those we deem to be different. The result is an evocative and inspiring book that teaches us important lessons about compassion, inclusivity and ultimately, finding the courage to overcome fear and follow our dreams."

—Carol Shaben, author of *Into the Abyss*

"This is a small story, a local story, an intimate story that McFarlane, with her honesty, clarity and intelligence, opens into a narrative that will widen your world, stretch your heart, and spark your curiosity, not just for people you meet with Down syndrome, but for everyone you meet. *Writing With Grace* makes you want to tear down walls and embrace life."

—Claudia Casper, author of *The Reconstruction*

Chapter 1

Once upon a time there is a lady call Cinderella — GRACE WEi JU CHEN. CG is 23 year old she has a stright jet black hair! Also she has a jet black eyes, and she has a jet red rose gloss lips. She has a very soft and smooth silky face! Her father is very rich and so does her real mother, during the winter my real mother had just died. Then when I turn ⟶ ⟹ around and I saw my stepmother looking an evil, mean eyes at me I was crying beside my real mother's bed! The two evil and ugly scary stepsisters, and they are standing closed to their mother. Cinderella mom's room is very dark, and there is only one light candle beside the

Writing with Grace

A Journey beyond
DOWN SYNDROME

Judy McFarlane

Douglas & McIntyre

Douglas & McIntyre (2013) Ltd.
P.O. Box 219
Madeira Park, BC, CANADA VON 2H0
www.douglas-mcintyre.com

Edited by Maureen Nicholson
Text design by Carleton Wilson
Cover design by Anna Comfort O'Keeffe and Carleton Wilson
Printed and bound in Canada

Cataloguing data available from Library and Archives Canada
978-1-77162-025-3 (paper)
978-1-77162-026-0 (ebook)

We gratefully acknowledge financial support from the Government of Canada through the Canada Book Fund and the Canada Council for the Arts, and from the Province of British Columbia through the BC Arts Council and the Book Publishing Tax Credit.

For
Grace,
Kathleen, my mother,
and Kathleen, my daughter

•••

Once upon a time, there was me.

—Grace Chen, *Cinderella-Grace, Vancouver Princess*

Is it not the life undertaking of all of us... to become human? It can be a long and sometimes painful process. It involves a growth to freedom, an opening up of our hearts to others, no longer hiding behind masks or behind the walls of fear or prejudice. It means discovering our common humanity.

—Jean Vanier, *Becoming Human*

CONTENTS

PART ONE

Impossible

THE NOTEBOOK LIES unopened on the table in front of us.

"You can read it," Grace says.

A square of paper taped to the front cover tells me otherwise: *Stay AWAY! Do Not Read!!*

"Are you sure?"

Grace slides the notebook closer to me. "It's okay with me."

I open the front cover and turn the pages. Titles jump out: *How to Be a Spy. Rules for Working.* Lists in neat, childish printing. A paragraph about riding the bus with a friend. A poem about love. Near the end, a number of blank pages. I'm about to close the book when my eye catches something on the last page. One sentence. I stare at the words. I can't believe they're here, in this notebook.

I always dream to be a famous writer.

• • •

THE CALL CAME out of the blue.

My friend Madelyne, head of the Caring Ministry at a local church. "She's about twenty-three or -four and has Down syndrome. Her name is Grace. She does a lot of volunteering here—" Madelyne paused, as if finding a tactful way to go on. "She—she's told me she really wants to go someplace besides her own backyard. And just a week ago, she said she wanted to write. A book. So I was wondering— would you talk to her? Just something about writing. Maybe help her get started?"

I hesitated. A picture was forming in my head—a heavy young woman staring at me with small, dull eyes. Someone who didn't look as though she could read, let alone write. "So you're saying she can read?"

"Grace loves to read. She's at about a grade five or six level, I think."

I was surprised. I'd never met anyone with Down syndrome. But in spite of that, or maybe because of it, the picture in my head was transforming into a dark, grainy film: a blank-eyed Grace staring at me as I tried over and over to make her understand some small point about writing; an agitated Grace abruptly standing up, looming over me, angry—

I shuddered, appalled at myself. And puzzled. Where had these images come from? Why did I feel a flat edge of fear pressing deep inside me?

But Madelyne was waiting for my answer. I'd known her since our sons, now in their late teens, had been in preschool together. She wouldn't ask something like this lightly.

"I don't know," I said, "if I could talk to Grace." Madelyne was silent.

"About writing, I mean. I'll have to think about it."

"Okay," Madelyne accepted my hesitation graciously. "If you decide you'd like to meet her, let me know."

Several weeks passed. I didn't call Madelyne. How could I tell her that our short conversation had triggered thoughts I was ashamed to admit? That Grace would be dull, possibly stupid. Unpredictable. Maybe dangerous. That I was afraid to meet her.

• • •

I REALIZED AFTER Madelyne's call that I knew nothing about Down syndrome. What causes it; what are people with it capable of doing; how do they manage their lives? My ignorance was complete. It was as if I'd never paid enough attention to really see anyone with the condition.

Down syndrome, I discovered, is the most common genetic defect, occurring about once in every eight hundred births. It's estimated that worldwide there are six million people with Down syndrome, with over four hundred thousand of those in the U.S. and thirty-five thousand in Canada. In 1958, the French geneticist Jérôme Lejeune and his team discovered the cause—an extra, or third, copy of the twenty-first chromosome. As a result, Down syndrome is also known as trisomy-21.

That extra chromosome, buried in every cell, can cause a cascade of difficulties—a lower than average IQ, delayed development, vision and hearing problems, obesity, digestive tract problems, leukemia, thyroid problems, infertility, speech problems, mobility and coordination issues, and congenital heart defects. People with Down syndrome also have an increased risk of developing autism, psychosis, depression, anxiety, and disruptive behaviour disorder.

Although some degree of intellectual disability occurs in everyone with Down syndrome, the other difficulties don't always occur. And the mental disability can range from mild to extreme. On the positive side, people with Down syndrome have lower rates of many cancers and rarely develop hardening of the arteries.

Until medical knowledge and techniques improved in the twentieth century, a child with Down syndrome seldom lived long enough to become a teenager. Even in the 1960s, the life expectancy of someone with Down syndrome was only twenty years. Today, many live past fifty, though they have a high risk of developing Alzheimer's disease.

Because Down syndrome can be detected, it has become the "poster child" for prenatal testing. Almost all developed countries provide screening tests, as well as more invasive diagnostic tests. A very high percentage of those who learn they're going to have a baby with Down syndrome choose to abort it. In Canada and the U.S., the rate of abortion of Down syndrome fetuses is estimated to be 85 percent, and it's even higher in some European countries. According to a 2012 article in the *Globe and Mail,* the number of people living with Down syndrome is projected to double by 2025 because those with Down syndrome now live so much longer.

In spite of this small expansion of my knowledge, I still felt uneasy. Based on what Madelyne had told me, I suspected that Grace's disability was mild. But that, in a way, increased my uneasiness. She might be more difficult to work with, more likely to become upset, agitated. The same small dark, grainy film began to play again in my head. No, I thought. This can't work. Grace was a shadowy figure, someone I couldn't see clearly. Someone I didn't want to see.

• • •

A WISP OF memory. So faint, so elusive, that when I try to bring it into focus, I can only see a faint picture, as if I'm viewing it from a long distance. A small, dark-haired girl walking along the main street of a small town. I can make out a couple of older boys who seem to be following a big girl. I stare at this slip of memory, trying to see more. The big girl has a funny way of walking, as if she's rolling from side to side. She jiggles with each step. She's holding one hand up in front of her. What's she doing? I stare and realize some long-forgotten memory has filled in the detail. She's the girl whose parents own the bakery; the girl who sometimes walks along with a doughnut on each finger, sugary edible rings. The girl whose face looks blank. I watch the boys call out to her, laughing. The big girl plods on, ignoring them. The small, dark-haired girl hangs back, watching, waiting to see what's going to happen next. The boys call out again, laughing. A word that lodges in the small girl's head. My head. *Retard.*

--- --- ---

SHE WANTS TO WRITE, Madelyne had said. How could someone like Grace imagine writing a book? How could she understand something as complex as writing? How could she even think of doing what I found so hard to do?

She wants to write.

The words snagged in me and refused to go away.

THE HOUSE ISN'T far from mine. I park on the street and walk along the driveway. Even though it's late April, the ground is cold. A chill wind blows up from English Bay. Near the front door, vivid clumps of blue flutter in an oval bed. Grape hyacinths. So blue. So hopeful. So reckless.

Another step and a voice wells up inside me. *Stop. You're making a big mistake.* I pause in the middle of the driveway and pretend to fish something out of my bag. *What makes you think she'll be able to understand you? Or that you'll be able to understand her? For all you know, she could be unpredictable, even dangerous.*

Willing myself to ignore the voice, I walk to the front door and raise my hand, ready to knock. The voice kicks up the volume, insisting that I pay attention. *Now,* it says. *Leave now!*

From the street, I hear a deep *woof* as a neighbour walks by with her large dog. Abruptly I see myself as she must—a woman frozen at the front door, hand raised. Just walk away, I tell myself. Who would know I've been here, besides the unknown neighbour, one large dog, and me?

But I've agreed to meet Grace. If I leave, I'll never know what she's like. I'll never find out if she can write.

As I stand with my hand raised, frozen, the door opens. An Asian woman about my age smiles as she bows, a pair of pink terry-cloth slippers neatly clasped in one hand. Over her shoulder peeks a slender girl who looks about twelve. Pretty, though her eyes are hidden by the glint from her wire-frame glasses.

"Hi," I say. "I'm Judy. Madelyne said—"

"Yes, yes. I am Jessica." The Asian woman bobs again, smiling broadly now as she turns to her daughter. "And this is Grace."

Grace looks up, her eyes dark and intense. "Hi," she says. "How's it going?"

I force myself to look at Grace, to smile, and suddenly shy, she ducks her head, her shoulder-length black hair swinging forward before she looks up again. She giggles, poking a finger in her mother's side. "I'm going to get you," she sings in a low voice, her face close to her mother's ear.

"Grace." Jessica pushes her daughter's hand away. "That is not polite." A tinge of annoyance in her voice.

I step into the front hall, onto the clean white tiles of the entrance and slip off my shoes. The spongy pink slippers now sit on the floor. As I slip my feet into them, I feel an unfamiliar softness, as if my feet were strangers here, too. I shift my bag on my shoulder and Grace motions me to follow her. She leads me across the gleaming wooden floors of the living room, where the sofa, chairs, and upright piano are all draped in clear plastic, to the dining room. A plastic-covered table is covered with neat piles of papers, notebooks, and an assortment of pens and pencils laid out in a precise order. Two chairs sit side by side, facing a wide window. Outside, the dark, gnarled branches of an old fruit tree bounce with each gust of wind. Grace sits down and pats the other chair, not looking at me. She's nervous, I realize. Like I am.

As I sit down, Grace makes some minute adjustments to her rows of pens and pencils, lining them up in an even more precise order. I sense this display of precision is important in some way I don't yet understand. And that it gives Grace another few seconds before we begin.

"Madelyne tells me you'd like to write." Grace, head down, nods to the table.

"A book?" Another nod.

"What do you want to write?"

Grace whispers to the table, "Cinderella."

I feel a sharp disappointment. Isn't this a story that has had every possible variation wrung out of it? Stifling my disappointment, I ask, "What will your Cinderella look like?"

Grace looks up at me, her face suddenly alive. "I'll show you." She jumps up, disappearing into the hallway and up the stairs. In a moment she returns, holding up a dark, almost blue-black velvet dress. "This." She clears her throat. "This is what I'll wear." Grace giggles and gives a small hop. The hem of her dress flies up, as if it's excited too.

I'm stunned. Does she want to tell her own story? "Such a deep blue, almost black," I finally say.

"Yes." Grace runs her tongue over her lower lip. "It's—it's Titanic blue."

I smile. Grace's use of the word *Titanic* perfectly captures the colour of her dress. And she has no way of knowing my connection to that word. How my father's family had tickets to sail on the *Titanic* and had to forfeit them when my father's baby sister developed the measles.

"What happens in your story?"

Grace pushes her dark hair behind her ears, revealing two identical hearing aids. "Well, my real mother dies." She giggles and glances toward the adjacent kitchen, where Jessica's making tea and, I suspect, listening intently. Grace's thoughts bubble out in fragments. "My father remarries my mean stepmother. Two evil, mean stepdaughters. The fairy godmother. I go to the ball. I find my prince!"

I realize we've entered the well-worn territory I'd hoped to avoid. "What else?" I ask.

"We go for our honeymoon on the *Titanic* and—"

"The *Titanic!*" I turn in my chair so I can look at Grace. Does she understand what she's saying? "Do you know what happened to the *Titanic?*"

Grace sighs, an unspoken "Duh!" hanging in the air. "It hit an iceberg and sunk."

"So what happens to you and your prince?"

"We get rescued by the royal helicopter and go to the Beverly Hills Hotel. Have a break!" Grace laughs. "Then I have three babies. All girls. And my prince and me, we become famous international spies."

"Anything else?"

"That's all for this book. In the second one, we go into space."

I lean back, stunned into silence once more. Grace's story is clear in her mind. She has a story, her story, and she knows how she wants to tell it.

"How do you want to start?"

Grace stares at me for a moment, running her tongue across her lower lip. "How about 'Once upon a time'?"

Bending over her lined notebook, she clicks her mechanical pencil and carefully begins to print.

Once upon a time there was a lady called Cinderella-Grace.
She is twenty-three years old and has straight jet-black hair! She
has jet black eyes, and jet red rose gloss lips.

After an intense hour of Grace writing and me asking
questions and giving writing prompts, I say, "I have to leave
now, Grace."

"Will you—are you coming back?" She glances up at me,
a quick, shy glance.

I pick up my pen and bend down to pick up my bag. I'm
stalling, I know. Can I do this? I don't know. Some of my
fears have vanished. I think Grace and I can talk. Her eyes
are not the least bit dull. She's not angry or agitated. But I
don't know if I can do this. I glance up to see Grace is still
focused on me, waiting for my answer. "Is next Friday a
good day for us to meet?" I ask.

Grace calls out, her voice loud and harsh. "Mom! Is next
Friday a good day to meet?"

Jessica enters from the kitchen. "Yes," she says, "next Friday is a good day. But you don't need to yell, Grace."

Grace thumps her elbows on the table. "Jeez. I was just
asking."

●　●　●

AS I LEAVE Grace's house, walking back along the driveway,
a thought gnaws at me. Could Grace possibly see herself as
Cinderella, as someone who will be transformed from the
slow sister into the princess? And if she does, what does that
mean? Does she think that writing her story will force the
rest of us, like the evil stepmother and her ugly daughters,
to see her as she really is? Or as she wants to be seen? That
writing will carry her out of the shadow of her disability into
the bright light of recognition?

This writing, Grace writing, could set up impossible expectations. Huge disappointment is a real possibility. What am I doing? My one visit has shown me how wrong I was when Madelyne first asked me to talk to Grace. She's not remotely close to what I'd imagined. She's someone who can imagine a story; someone who can find a word like *Titanic* to describe a blue-black dress.

If I do this, I start to think. If. What am I thinking? I don't know if I want to do this. Or if I can do this. I feel the same edge of fear pressing into me that I'd felt when Madelyne called me.

DURING THE WEEK, I rehearse calling Grace's mother Jessica and telling her I can't continue. *I'm sorry*, I begin. But what comes after feels like flimsy bits of truth, half-lies—my family needs me, I have other projects on the go. I know I can't say to Jessica what I really think: that helping her daughter write a book is an impossible idea. I have serious doubts whether I can write a book, so how can someone like Grace do this? Impossible. But how do you say impossible to a mother like Jessica who's probably heard that word many times?

• • •

THE NEXT FRIDAY, as I settle into the chair beside Grace at her dining room table, a cup of hot oolong tea beside me, Grace shows me what she's done. Ten more pages, neatly printed in her notebook.

Grace fiddles with her line of pens and pencils, making minute adjustments to their positions.

"I'll just take a minute to read this, okay?" I say.

"Can you read it out loud?" Grace says.

I nod and begin:

Back at the white castle, Cinderella-Grace helps her stepsisters with their gowns. It is time for the ball. "Well, Cinderella," her stepmother sneered with a laugh, "you are not ready yet. What a shame, hnh."

As I read, I feel Grace nudge her chair closer to mine. Although Grace's writing is only loosely fixed in the present tense, there's a strong dramatic element to it:

My stepsisters go to the ball with their mother, leaving me all alone in the white castle! I covered my face with both my hands together, and her body shakes so hard she just can't stop it.

I stop and take a sip of my tea, cooled now. The story is there; it's the details that need work.

"We need to talk about some writing things," I say. "You know what I mean when I say 'the present tense'?" I look at Grace. Does she understand? Is this a sham we're going through?

Grace nods, a serious look on her face. "That's—that's now?"

"Yes! That's it. So when you say 'my stepsisters go to the ball,' that's in the present, but then you say 'I covered my face,' that's in the—"

"Past! That's the past." Grace glances up at me as if she's wondering why we're sidetracked on this.

"So you need to make them all agree. Make your story either in the past or in the present. Will you do that for next week?"

"Yeah, sure." Grace nods, slightly impatient, as if to tell me let's not get bogged down on this.

Surprised, I decide to tackle the other glaring problem, point of view. "You see, how sometimes you say 'she,' and other times you say 'I'?"

Grace nods again, the same serious look.

"So you can decide which one it is," I say. "It's called point of view, POV. It can be either one, *she* or *I*."

Grace takes a loud sip from her glass of juice. "She or I." She looks up at me. "I'm not sure," she says.

"Okay, why don't you think about it?"

Grace nods, and we carry on, slowly working our way through her printed pages. We only make it to page five when I realize an hour has passed and I have to go.

A FEW DAYS earlier, I'd noticed a poster advertising *Cinderella: The Musical*. It was going to be performed at a theatre about a forty-five-minute drive from where Grace lived. Was it worth driving that far to see something that might be boring or mediocre? And what if Grace became upset or angry while we were far from her home? What if she decided she didn't want to stay with me and took off? How would I handle that? Grace hadn't given me any reason at all to think this way, but I did. The image I'd thought of when Madelyne called me was, I realized, still close to the surface, waiting to pop up when I least expected it.

AT THE DOOR, as I pull on my shoes, Grace leans against the wall. "Any plans for the weekend?" I ask.

"Not really. Sometimes I watch a movie with my dad." She giggles. "Sometimes he falls asleep! Jeez."

Jessica appears and hands me my jacket. "Next Friday is okay?" Her face is open and pleasant, revealing nothing. But just now I wonder if what I hear is a bit of hope in her voice that I'll want to continue working with her daughter. I suddenly sense how so much of what I take for granted, and what my children, only a few years younger than Grace, take for granted, is not easy for Grace or Jessica.

"Friday's good for me," I say and turn to Grace. "More pages?"

Grace giggles and pushes herself off the wall, giving me a high-five. "More pages."

LATER THAT DAY when I get home, I call Jessica. "I forgot to mention something today. There's going to be a play, a musical, about Cinderella next week. Do you think Grace would like to go?"

THE NIGHT OF the play, as I pull into Grace's driveway, her front door flings open and Grace runs toward me. She opens the car door and jumps into the passenger seat. "Hi! How are you? Can we go? Let's go!" She giggles and bounces on the seat. In the soft light of the early evening, I see Jessica at the front door, waving and motioning to me to make sure Grace does up her seat belt. As I turn to Grace, she snaps her belt into place and rolls down her window. She leans her head out as far as she can and yells, "Don't do anything silly, okay, Mom!"

At the theatre, Grace and I settle into our seats. As the lights dim, Grace pulls out her notebook, pen, and a small penlight, flicking it on. She leans into me. "I want to make some notes about the play," she whispers in a loud voice. I nod. No one is sitting beside us, so I think the small light won't bother anyone. But in a few minutes an usher taps Grace on her shoulder and very firmly asks her to turn out her light. Grace looks up at me, the light abruptly shining up on both our faces. For a second I wonder if this is the moment I'd feared, the one where Grace flares out of control. I lean close to her and whisper, "It makes it hard for people to see. Can you turn it out?"

"Oh," she says and turns it off. She stuffs her light and notebook back in her bag and from that moment focuses on the stage. In the final scene, as the prince takes Cinderella tenderly in his arms, Grace sits riveted, staring at the stage long after the applause fades.

ON THE WAY out we stop by the stage door, hoping that some of the principals, maybe Cinderella herself, will appear to sign autographs. But as the crowd thins and no one appears, I finally say we need to leave. Reluctantly, we squeeze into the elevator with the last stragglers, one of them a young man with Down syndrome. Grace glances at him then up at me. "Cool," she says.

By now it's past eleven, and heavy rain has turned the road into a slick ribbon. I grip the wheel tightly, concentrating on making it home safely. The car's quiet, a comfortable kind of quiet.

As we move through the darkness, Grace begins to sing. Her voice low, almost a monotone, but full of energy. I recognize the tune as one of the songs from the performance we've just seen, but the noise of the rain and the car muffle her words. Whatever the words are, Grace is singing them over and over.

I listen intently. It sounds like Grace is singing "I'm paused a little," but that can't be right. I listen again and finally I get it. Grace is singing "Impossible," the song Cinderella sings as she realizes she will be able to go to the ball after all.

I glance sideways. Grace's eyes are closed, her arms stretching out in front of her. I realize she's singing to an audience I can't see, one beyond the dark, rain-slicked window. An audience that's asking her to sing her song, over and over.

IMPOSSIBLE.

PART TWO

I Want to Write

GRACE HAD SAID, "I want to write." The very words that I couldn't say to anyone when I was her age. What I still found hard to say.

●●●

IT'S EARLY OCTOBER of my second year at the University of British Columbia. I feel as though I'm treading water, not going anywhere. My classes are a hodgepodge—an introductory course on Chaucer, where we struggle through the *Canterbury Tales* and memorize bits of Middle English; a small class in conversational French, where we have puzzling conversations as we confuse *cheveux*/hair with *chevaux*/ horses; a second-year Spanish course, where I write a poem about a drop of water falling from an olive tree, something I've never seen. I find my classes stimulating, but I know they're not taking me where I want to go. I want to learn how to write.

For as long as I can remember, whatever I've done, I've also watched: compulsively reading facial expressions, noting details, describing it all to myself. Words and sentences jammed my brain. As I grew up, my running commentary, something I couldn't seem to stop, started to feel strange. As if I were me and at the same time someone else, observing myself and everyone around me. If I can learn to write, I tell myself, I'll be able to pull those sentences out of my head and start to make sense of them.

I STOP OUTSIDE the blue-and-white building. This is it, Buchanan Block E, the place I've been searching for. I ease my heavy bag off my shoulder onto the ground and stare at the black letters on the glass door: Creative Writing, Fourth Floor. The door is aluminum-framed, dull grey, mesh-embedded glass. I reach out and grasp the smudged grey handle.

Alongside the building, a line of trees bursts with brilliant yellow, as if lit from within. I hear a rustle, the faint sound of a brittle leaf landing on the pavement.

But as I stand there an impossible-to-ignore voice wells up in my head. *What makes you think you have something to say?* I try to block the voice, pretending I don't hear it. But it speaks again, more loudly. *What makes you think you can be a writer?* I drop my hand.

OUR WARM KITCHEN, the radio on. *Kindergarten of the Air.* Every weekday morning, my mother and I listen to it. She's set up a small table and chair beside the fridge with some paper, crayons and pencils. I sit there while the program plays, listening to the letter and number of the day. Today it's B and 4. My mother kneads a big floury round of dough on the green linoleum counter.

As the program ends, I hold up my paper and point to a line of uneven printing. *"B-B-B-B-B-B."* I say the sound fast, almost a buzz.

My mother laughs and walks over to me, wiping her hands on her apron. "Look at these too," she says, pointing to my uncertain 4s. She kneels down close to me, suddenly serious, and cups my face in her hands. They're warm and strong and dry with bits of flour. "What do you want to be when you grow up?" she asks. "You can be anything you want."

I stare at her. I know she's saying something important, though I don't really know what it is. But I understand that she believes in me. That out in the world, the place beyond our small town, there are unlimited possibilities waiting for me. That I can be something.

LATER, WHEN I'M old enough to understand, my mother tells me more of her story. How at fourteen, she had to drop out of school during the Depression to help her parents in their fruit orchard. How she didn't return to school and, at nineteen, married my father. As my brothers and I grew up, she only rarely talked about returning to school, as if by then it was something far beyond her reach. But she was a voracious reader and she often told me she wanted to write a book one day. But she didn't write. It was a dream. Nothing more.

NOW, AS I stand in front of the building I've searched for, I stare at the door. What am I doing here, unable to open it? In some way I can't put into words, I know my mother's dream is here. For a second, I see her face as she tells me I can be anything. *If I fail,* I think, but I don't let myself finish the thought. Those words linger. *If I fail.*

Finally, I pick up my bag and begin the long walk back to my residence. Kick a few leaves, scuff my feet along the gravel path. Disappointment falls over me, like an old coat.

● ● ●

AND THERE WAS something else. A memory still so vivid it felt like a sharp blade slicing through me.

The night after graduation from high school, a night when we thought the world glowed in front of us, we were woken by a phone call in the early morning. There'd been an accident. Near the lake. On the way home from an after-grad party. Five dead. No, three. Six? The numbers bounced around in the early hours as we waited.

My brother John and I are in our basement, waiting. John, who repeated grade eleven and is graduating with me, paces back and forth beside the weights he works out on most days after school. I sit on the wooden stairs my mother painted a bright red, staring at the jars of canned fruit she's lined up on the shelves at one end of the stairs. Peaches, pears, plums; jars of yellow, white, deep red. John is sure his best friend Michael was at the party, one my mother had forbidden us from attending.

We wait. There's nothing to say. The phone rings again upstairs and our father picks up. His voice low. *Yes. I see. Thanks.* A math and physics teacher at the high school, he's taught almost every student who's graduating. He could tell you who was bright but would go "down the hill" to the smelter instead of to university; who never got algebra but always showed up on time. We hear him walk to the top of the stairs, the door opening. I feel the stairs shake as he comes down past me and stands beside the washing machine. He holds his mouth in a funny line and turns his head half away from us. *Seven,* he says. *They think it was head on.* He stops, as if sorting the details. *A dump truck. They think they crossed over the centre line. It was—*He lists the names we will hear over and over in the next few weeks. Then he starts back up the stairs. Halfway up, he pauses. *Come upstairs,* he says. *Mum's made some tea.* He adds, knowing we haven't taken it all in, *Michael wasn't there.*

That night was the first time I heard the universe hiss, a sound like an icy flare. *What makes you think you can escape this small place? That you can be someone? Just who do you think you are?*

I tried to pretend I hadn't heard that hiss. But it lodged somewhere deep inside me. Waiting.

●●●

FRIDAY AFTERNOON. I'M at Grace's dining room table, her notebook and pens and pencils lined up in the same precise order. And something I haven't seen before—an old, dark leather-covered photo album. As Jessica sets a thermos of tea and a cup down beside me, Grace flips open the album.

"Me," she begins without preamble, her finger landing on a black-and-white studio portrait. "When I was a baby," she adds, in case I don't understand. She turns the page. "Albert and me." Grace is less than two and her brother, Albert, a bright-eyed baby. Another page. "Me, in grade one. The first day!" Grace exhales noisily. "I love my teacher!" The photo shows a small class sitting in two neat rows, Grace in front, near the centre. The teacher, a young woman, stands at the side, smiling in the moment of stillness.

Grace's face darkens as she turns the page to a formal family portrait. She jabs her finger down on an older man, clearly the patriarch. "My grandfather," she says, her voice low. "He said *Down,* right to my face! Jeez!" She slaps the album shut and stares out the window. Anger floods out from her, washing over the table, her notebooks, me.

"Grace." I don't know what to say except the obvious. "You don't like the word *Down?*"

"No! I hate that word." She continues to stare out the window, refusing to look at me.

GRACE'S INTENSE REACTION to the word *Down* puzzles me. It seems a neutral word, nothing like the derogatory words and labels that are sometimes used even today. And where did *Down* come from?

In the middle of the 1800s, when words like *lunatic* and *idiot* were considered medical terms, a young British doctor, John Langdon Down, became the medical director of an institution called the Royal Earlswood Asylum for Idiots. Langdon Down knew almost nothing about "idiots," and the asylum had recently run afoul of the British Lunacy Commission, forcing the previous director to abruptly resign. Langdon Down was brilliant—he'd walked away with most of the big prizes as a medical student—but poor. Then he was offered this position that paid 150 pounds a year. It was not a lot, but enough to support him and the woman he hoped to marry, Mary Crellin.

In his first week at the asylum, John Langdon Down was afraid he'd made a terrible mistake. The records of patient admissions and treatment were almost non-existent. Some rooms of the asylum were dirty and stained. Some outside areas little more than a field of muck. Some buildings had no heat. There was a problem with bedwetting and soiling. Some of the staff drank too much. And there were over two hundred residents to look after.

But Langdon Down stuck with his new position. Mary visited often during the first year and within a couple of years they were married. Together they began to make the changes that would set Earlswood apart as a model institution: training programs to improve coordination and speech, improved diet, and a schedule for meals. Most important to both John and Mary was treating the residents with respect.

Langdon Down was appalled to see when he first arrived that meals were rude affairs: bread and butter piled up on greasy tablecloths; cups dipped into communal jugs. Some of the new residents, he observed, were humiliated by what they saw.

With Mary's help, he began to make wholesale changes. Meals would be served on plates. Tea would arrive in tea-pots and be poured into cups with saucers. "The worst cases" would eat in another room, so they could get the help they needed and not disturb the others. The residents would be expected to obey the rules but would be treated as if they were family. The staff would be held to a high standard—physical punishment was strictly forbidden.

IN A LECTURE some years later called "The Education and Training of the Feeble in Mind," Langdon Down revealed a deep sympathy for his residents:

> The first thing was to rescue them from loneliness, to give them some companionship ... to surround them with the influences of art and nature, to bring some joy to their lives, to stimulate them, to make them think.

As Langdon Down got to know his young residents, he became fascinated with those of one group in particular. Their almond-shaped eyes and flattened features made them look Asiatic, but their parents were British. How could that be? He began to photograph each resident and take careful cranial measurements in the hopes of discovering a system of classifying the feeble-minded. He was convinced they "were always congenital idiots, and never result[ed] from accidents after uterine life."

A theory popular at the time classified all humans into five ethnic categories. Although Langdon Down observed examples of all categories among his residents, he focused in "Observations of an Ethnic Classification of Idiots" on the "Mongolian" type:

> A very large number of congenital idiots are typical Mongols. The hair is not black, as in the real Mongol, but of a brownish colour, straight and scanty. The face is flat and broad, and destitute of prominence. The cheeks are roundish, and extended laterally. The eyes are obliquely placed ... The lips are large and thick, with transverse fissures. The tongue is long, thick, and is much roughened. The nose is small.

At the time Langdon Down was puzzling over his observations, the science of genetics was virtually unknown. Slavery was still practised in some places, and many believed that a clear hierarchy existed among the races of man, with Caucasians, no surprise, at the top of the heap. There was even doubt that all humans were related.

Siding with those who believed that all humans were related, Langdon Down suggested that his young patients were a step backward in evolution, an example of the more highly developed Caucasian race regressing to the less-developed Mongolian race. He called them "Mongolian idiots."

Some scientists scoffed at the name almost as soon as Langdon Down suggested it, but it caught on. For over one hundred years, those like Grace were known as Mongoloids, Mongols, or Mongolian idiots.

So how did that name disappear and *Down syndrome* become the term everyone uses today?

In 1961 a group of scientists decided the term *Mongolian idiot* was not only misleading, it was also embarrassing, particularly for the Chinese and Japanese scientists working in the field. The group wrote to the editor of *The Lancet*, the leading British medical journal, suggesting alternative names, three of which contained the word *Down* in honour of the man who had first recognized the condition. Twenty leading experts from North America, Europe and Japan, including Langdon Down's grandson, Dr. Norman Langdon Down, signed the letter. After much deliberation, *The Lancet*'s editor announced that *Mongolism* would become known, for the time being, as *Down's syndrome,* in recognition of John Langdon Down. When the condition was better understood, he said, a new name would be considered.

But in spite of this pronouncement, the old names persisted. *Mongoloid, Mongol.* The public as well as many doctors continued to use them. Four years later, in 1965, the Mongolian People's Republic approached the World Health Organization, asking it to drop all references to Mongoloids. That term, they said, was especially insulting to them. WHO quickly adopted *Down's syndrome* as the official term.

Even so, the term *Mongoloid* continued to be used for at least a couple of decades (and sporadically much later: at one event I attended with Grace, an elderly woman leaned close to me and said in a low voice, "Such a wonderful little Mongoloid!").

Very slowly, *Down's syndrome* has won out. But that name has had its own small controversy—a grammatical one. A group of American scientists argued that the possessive was wrong: the condition should be called *Down syndrome.* Those in Britain stuck with *Down's syndrome,* whereas Canadians, for reasons unknown, adopted *Down syndrome.*

• • •

DOWN. WHY DOES Grace react so intensely to this seemingly neutral word? To her, it's as offensive as *Mongoloid* is to me.

"When Grace was born," Jessica says, "her colour was very rich. But the next day the doctor told us her spine felt soft and he suspected Down syndrome. At my university in Taipei, I studied genetics. So right away the pictures from the textbook come into my mind. Grace has a DNA test, and one month later the diagnosis is confirmed."

"For seven years we try to have a baby," Jessica continues. "David is the eldest son. There was a lot of pressure. We almost gave up when I learn I am pregnant. I was overjoyed. David laughed at me and said, 'Why don't you take out a big ad in the newspaper? Tell everyone!' When we got the diagnosis, my world shut down. But David says, 'Crying doesn't make any help. Now we have to think how to help this child.'"

She paused, adding, "David's father, he told David to put Grace in an institution. To forget her. Then we decide. We will move far away, make a new life."

As I listen to Jessica tell me this part of Grace's story, I begin to understand Grace's reaction. She understands that her grandfather used the word *Down* to convey that there was no place for Grace in his family and that he saw no place for her in the outside world.

• • •

I AVOIDED WRITING for a long time after I turned away from that door at university. I pretended I didn't pay close attention to details, recording them, turning them into sentences that bumped around in my head. In my third year of university, I abandoned my English studies and applied to law school. Surprisingly, I was accepted. Law, I told myself, was something I could do, even though I knew very little about it and had never encountered a lawyer. Law was practical and would let me earn a living. Unlike writing. Early on, I realized I seemed to fall short on something most of my classmates relished: an ability to engage in the back and forth of a biting argument. For some of them, the more aggressive the argument, the greater the degree of verbal conflict, the more they enjoyed it.

I attributed my aversion to the shyness I'd always had, something I would eventually grow out of. One day, I told myself, I'd be able to argue as fiercely as anyone. Although my aversion to argument and conflict made me uneasy, without any other clear options I stuck with law school, graduating and finding employment with a small firm that represented musicians and bands. From there I moved to a corporate legal office, where I began to work on large contract negotiations. By then, writing—the creative kind— hovered between faint memory and lost dream. Not gone altogether, but no longer something I thought I'd do. I was different now: someone who had to lay out the facts, work through both sides of an argument, and find the places that might give during negotiations. Words were my tools, but they had to be stripped of any possibility of uncertainty. Nuance and subtlety were banished, replaced, I hoped, by certainty and precision. For ten years I managed to create a believable version of myself as someone who could do what was required.

■ ■ ■

IN MY MID-THIRTIES, my biological clock clanging, I had three children in four years. I returned to work only a couple of months after our first son was born, but when our second son was born eighteen months later, I had some complications and wasn't able to return to work as soon as I'd planned. As my maternity leave stretched out, I realized I had no desire to leave our two small boys. And by then, I'd begun to accept that conflict, especially on a daily basis, made me very uncomfortable.

It had dawned on me as I observed our children and their small friends play that I was a classic middle child, wanting to avoid conflict. Although I'd done a lot of negotiating, and liked it, I knew that even the smoothest negotiations sometimes tipped into conflict and confrontation. The long and unpredictable hours that my work often required only added to the stress.

By this time, the business that my husband, Jim, had started just after we married was on stronger footing. As the business started to produce a reliable income, I stopped practising law and became a full-time mother. The transition was a bumpy one. As a lawyer, I was used to people listening to me, respecting my opinion, whether I deserved that or not. As a full-time mum I may as well have been just another dummy washing diapers and wiping up baby spit, with nothing interesting to say. Worse, I often felt like an invisible dummy. Several of my friends had gone through the same transition. Sometimes we'd laugh at our tumble in status. But it also angered me. Being a full-time mother was infinitely harder in many ways than practising law. And more important. But no one wanted to hear us say that. Or much else, it seemed.

∙ ∙ ∙

IN MY MID-FORTIES, my mother was diagnosed with an incurable form of slow-moving cancer and my father began to slide into dementia. My own mortality abruptly sprang into clear view. I woke up one morning with a number in my head. Thirty. The number of years I'd live if I was lucky. Once, time had stretched over the horizon into infinity. Now it sucked itself into a clearly visible finish line. In that waking moment, forever vanished. "Too late" loomed like a dark creature hunkered down on the horizon, coolly gazing back at me.

That fall I enrolled in a first-year writing course at the local community college, Capilano College. But as I drove up the hill for the first time, a wave of doubt engulfed me. What was I doing trying this at my age? What would my classmates, sure to be mostly eighteen- and nineteen-year-olds, some of whom might even know my teenaged children, think? I considered turning around, driving home and forgetting the whole ridiculous idea. But I knew what turning around felt like. I gripped the wheel and continued up the hill.

In my class, I wrote about my father losing his memory. I described his path from awareness of his loss—"I used to be smart," he told me one day as he gave up playing a game of Clue with my children—to confusion and anxiety as he badgered my mother over and over to tell him when they'd sold their house and what she'd done with the money. I described the sign my mother, desperate for relief from the constant questioning, had taped to the front of their fridge:

WE LIVE HERE NOW
THIS IS OUR HOME

I struggled to find the words to describe the moment when my father, standing in front of the fridge, ran his finger over my mother's words, trying to make sense of them. How he turned to me, someone I suspected he thought was a friendly stranger, his blue eyes anxious, and asked, "We live here now?"

I read what I had written about my father to my class, who turned out to be almost all the eighteen- and nineteen-year-olds I'd imagined. They listened and made suggestions. Some of them cried. In turn, I listened to the poems and stories that spilled out of them almost every class, many of them about young, thwarted, desperate, occasionally thrilling love. Sometimes I suggested small changes, but mostly I listened, bowled over by their innocence, their belief in themselves, and the wonder of life.

No one except me cared how old I was. It was my writing that mattered. Our teacher, Crystal Hurdle, bathed us in enthusiasm, prodding us in every class to write, write more. Two-thirds of the way through that first term, my mother's health took a serious turn for the worse. I left my husband and three children and travelled four hundred miles to be with her for what turned out to be the last two months of her life.

While I was with my parents, I did what I'd always done. I described to myself what was happening: the way my mother's hands felt bony and cool; the way my father, in his blue-and-white striped pyjamas, shuffled around the apartment, his slippers making a sound like fine sandpaper on the wooden floor. Some time later I knew I'd want to sort through these details, turn them over, so I could try to make sense of what had happened.

WHEN I FINALLY returned home, I was numb, exhausted. I returned to my class, but only a few weeks remained until the end of the term. It was impossible to make up what I'd missed. Reluctantly, I withdrew from my course.

The next fall, I enrolled in the same class again with the same teacher. I wrote a thinly disguised story about a woman roughly my age coming to grips with the loss of her mother. The details I'd stored up when I was with my mother spilled out in a messy sprawl. I tried to find words that described my grief, trying out one then another and finally comparing it to a flat grey sea, one I'd waded so far into I could no longer see the shore. I pretended my story was fiction and so did my teacher. My writing, I knew, was awkward, a beginner's writing. But there was something strangely comforting about letting the final moments of my mother's life seep out on the page. It was almost as if I was telling my mother a story the way I had when I was small, trying to get the details right, so we would both understand.

AT THE TIME Madelyne asked me to meet with Grace to see if I could help her get started writing, I was about to finish a master's program in creative writing. After my double dose of first-year writing courses at the local community college, I'd taken a couple of undergraduate creative writing courses at UBC in the same blue-and-white building I'd been unable to walk into when I was young. One of my teachers encouraged me to continue and I applied to the MFA program. Although I was rejected the first time, I was accepted on my second try. But my elation soon flatlined into serious doubt about whether I had what it took to be a writer. Although I managed to cobble together a book of linked short stories,

I knew what a novice I was and that it would take years to master the craft of writing, if I ever did.

So when Madelyne called to ask if I'd meet with Grace, I was at a low point. I knew I wanted to write. But whether I could was something I still had serious doubts about.

■ ■ ■

FRIDAY AFTERNOON. WHEN I arrive, Jessica tells me Grace is in her room changing her clothes. I think I catch a slight roll of her eyes. I smile and tell her that I've lost count of the times my daughter Kathleen decided to change moments before we were about to leave the house.

As we wait for Grace to appear, Jessica picks up Grace's childhood story from where she'd left it at my last visit. It would take several years for Jessica and David to receive the papers needed to immigrate to Canada. In the meantime Grace started preschool. "When Grace was three," Jessica tells me, "she went to the Swan Shi Developmental Institute in Taipei. Usually they take the students at age four, but they accepted Grace at a younger age because they thought she had potential. Then when she was six, we applied to a famous kindergarten, the one her brother Albert had gone to for a year," Jessica smiles. "They told us Grace could not go, because they could not accept the responsibility. So Grace went to a different kindergarten. After that, we found a principal at a regular school, someone who understand someone like Grace, and Grace started there. Her grade one teacher, Lisa Lin, was very patient, and she encourage all the class to support Grace." Just before Grace was about to start grade six, the family moved from Taiwan to Vancouver. Grace began grade six at the local elementary school. "She didn't know any English, only the alphabet," Jessica says, "but she listen to phonetic tapes. I didn't want her to learn English in Taiwan and pick up a bad accent."

Grace learned English quickly, and elementary school became a happy place for her, where she soon had friends.

- - -

JESSICA DIDN'T HAVE the amniocentesis test that would have given David and her a choice before Grace was born. Their choice, after her birth, was either to accept David's father's advice to put Grace away in an institution, or, as David said, to "think how to help this child."

At thirty-eight, when I became pregnant for a third time, my doctor recommended amniocentesis. At that time, the less invasive tests that exist today had not been developed. My doctor, a woman about my age, had asked me if I wanted to know the gender of my baby. With two small and very energetic boys already, I said yes. When I went to hear the results of my ultrasound, my doctor surprised me by putting her arm around me in the small examining room. "It's a girl," she said, her smile strangely muted. "But you have a complication." The ultrasound had also detected that the placenta had positioned itself to cover the cervix, blocking my baby's normal exit path. "It's called *placenta previa*," my doctor said. "We don't know why it happens, though it's much more common in older mothers."

She gave me strict instructions not to lift anything at all, particularly our boys, four and two. There was a brief bright spot when she said all vacuuming was out. If the placenta pulled away from the wall of the uterus, there was a high risk of massive and fatal hemorrhaging. Both my baby and I would likely die. If I noticed anything unusual—a bit of spotting, for example—I was to hightail it over the bridge to the hospital where she had privileges. Minutes would count at that point, she warned.

By the time I found myself lying on an examining table, blue-gowned, waiting for the doctor who would perform the amniocentesis, I knew enough to be worried. My high-risk pregnancy had led me to the books I'd never have found otherwise—books that described in painful detail what could go wrong with a pregnancy. I'd learned about gestational diabetes, eclampsia, and rare complications with twins, one not growing in order to give space to the other, or one even disappearing altogether.

And I'd read about the risks of the diagnostic test I was about to have, amniocentesis. Rarely, the needle injured the baby. Or the procedure could cause a tear in the amniotic sac allowing fluid to leak out, resulting in a smaller and smaller space for a growing baby. But at my advanced maternal age, the medical consensus was that these risks were unlikely compared to the dramatically increased risk of having a baby with a detectable defect. Such as Down syndrome.

The assistant squirted a line of cold gel onto my abdomen and smeared it with a gloved hand. Ultrasound would guide the needle safely into an empty pocket of fluid, carefully avoiding my baby. When the doctor entered the small room, he held what I now remember as a foot-long needle. He may have said those clichéd words "This won't hurt a bit," or not. It didn't matter. He was going to insert that needle into me and extract amniotic fluid to test for certain birth defects. Some of those I knew about from my expanded reading list—Down syndrome, Tay-Sachs, sickle-cell anemia—but I suspected there were many others I hadn't heard of. I tensed, willing myself to be motionless, breathing as lightly as possible as he slid the needle in, his eyes fixed on the ultrasound screen.

Out of the dark grainy shadows that seemed to hold nothing, an image abruptly appeared. A tiny being, a nub of life, placidly resting. My daughter. I knew if anything happened to her, at my advanced maternal age I probably wouldn't get another chance to try again.

I tried not to think about how my husband and I would deal with a serious defect. Neither of us was opposed to abortion on moral grounds, but—here, my intellectualizing broke down. This was a tiny being I already identified with, one I couldn't think about destroying. I prayed, in my apologetically agnostic way, for a smooth and boring procedure, for the dullness of normality.

My prayers, such as they were, were answered. Even though at my age, the chances of having a baby with Down syndrome had increased to 1 out of 125 (from 1 out of almost 1,700 at age twenty), we dodged the bullet with our daughter. No wrenching decisions, though, I can imagine, I think, what that would have felt like. We'd have weighed the welfare of our two small boys, my husband's more than full-time efforts to build a business, his dream since childhood, my own desire, intermittent and uncertain as it was, to have a career, against—against what? A child who would require immense effort, whose presence might cast a deep shadow over our boys, who might overwhelm our still developing and sometimes fragile family? A child who would likely always be a child, dependent on us, and when we were no longer around, on our sons. But a child. Our daughter.

We'd have wrestled back and forth, and I suspect nothing would have felt right. My doctor, who'd already told me that she didn't ever want to see me pregnant again, would, I suspected, have counselled abortion. Would we have agreed? I like to think now that we would have gone ahead with the pregnancy. But the truth is, I have no way of knowing. I do know that if that grainy ultrasound image, glimpsed for a few minutes, was my only memory of our daughter, I would have carried a deep sadness from that day forward.

∙ ∙ ∙

YEARS LATER, OUR daughter, Kathleen, who'd sailed through her high-risk beginning and was now in high school, arrived home one day with some news.

"Mum," she announced in the voice that always said, to me at least, pay attention, "you'll want to hear this!" I turned away from my laptop to look up at her.

"Remember Mrs. Goodwin?" she asked.

I stared at her, my brain unable to connect the name to any bit of memory.

"My teacher in grade four? *Harriet the Hamburger?*" Kathleen prompted.

Harriet. How could I possibly forget her? By now I'd struggled to write about Harriet for several years.

"Well—" Kathleen paused. She was a child born with a well-developed sense of dramatic flourish. "She had a baby."

"Mrs. Goodwin, not Harriet, right?"

"Oh, Mom." Kathleen grimaced, letting me know what a burden it was to have a mother with a cheesy sense of humour.

"What did she have?"

"A boy." Her phone buzzed and abruptly I ceased to exist as she headed down the hall to her room.

SEVERAL WEEKS LATER, I learned through the old mom grapevine that the baby was named Jack. And he had Down syndrome.

What's it like now for young parents of a baby with Down syndrome? I wondered. How was Kathleen's former teacher, one of her all-time favourites, managing?

One rainy evening, I found myself in the living room of Leanne and Harold Goodwin's spacious Vancouver home. I began by asking them about the day Jack was born.

"There were some start-up issues. With his breathing." Harold glanced at Leanne and added, "Once that was taken care of, I was joking, like, he looks Martian—" Harold abruptly leaned forward, elbows on knees, and dropped his gaze to the floor. In his late thirties, he was a trim, athletic-looking man. Leanne had told me he worked long hours in his family business, and his face revealed a deep tiredness.

"Maybe I didn't say it, the Martian thing. Maybe I only thought it," Harold said. "Our doctor took him to the warming table, and I started to feel it was taking too long, that something was wrong." He looked up. "Now, in hindsight, I know our doctor was composing herself, figuring out how to tell us."

Leanne took up the story. "She turned to us and said, 'You've got a special little guy here.' And then she said, 'Don't limit him.'"

Harold added, "It must have been after that that she said Down syndrome. It felt like something out of left field."

WHILE HAROLD AND Leanne's doctor would have had mere seconds to find words to describe their son, the question of how to characterize a baby or a fetus with Down syndrome has been the subject of fierce debate in Canada. Krista Flint, the former executive director of the Canadian Down Syndrome Society (CDSS), has said bluntly that a very high percentage of fetuses diagnosed with Down syndrome are aborted because of what doctors tell prospective parents. "Many families tell us that their doctor told them, 'Don't have this child. It will ruin your life.'"

In 2007, the Society of Obstetricians and Gynaecologists of Canada (SOGC) recommended that all women, regardless of age, be offered prenatal screening for Down syndrome. New non-invasive tests had been developed that screened for markers indicating a higher risk of "chromosomal abnormalities." All prospective mothers, the SOGC said, should be offered the choice of having these new tests. This was a big change: until then, screening was generally available only to women thirty-five or older at the time of delivery. Near the end of the list of SOGC recommendations for the new guidelines was this statement:

> Screening programs should show respect for the needs and quality of life of persons with disability. Counselling should be non-directive and should respect a woman's choice to accept or to refuse any or all of the testing or options offered at any point in the process.

Although that statement was clearly meant to address criticism like that raised by Krista Flint, the Canadian Down Syndrome Society objected, saying the new guidelines were rife with value-laden words such as *risk, defect, disorder, abnormal, anomaly*. All negative words. Why hadn't less judgmental words been used? *Difference, chance, probability*, for example.

AS I READ this exchange, I realized the argument was about something far more fundamental than words. Down syndrome, the CDSS maintained, was "not a birth defect or an illness," but "a naturally occurring chromosomal arrangement that has always been part of the human condition." At heart, it was an argument about what entry we allow a baby with Down syndrome to make into the world—already marked as genetically defective, or simply another variation in the wide spectrum of human possibilities.

The new less invasive tests only provided an estimate of the likelihood of a chromosomal problem when combined with the mother's age, ethnicity, and other factors, not a definite diagnosis. An assessment of high risk would lead to more decisions. Proceed to invasive tests? Carry to term even if a problem were detected? Or opt for abortion? And all these decisions would have to be made before the option for termination vanished, somewhere between weeks twenty and twenty-four.

Leanne continued. "And because I was under thirty-five, I didn't have an amnio. So we didn't know."

An abrupt cry startled us. Leanne glanced at Harold, who obligingly left the living room to investigate. Leanne refilled my cup of tea before continuing.

"When she said Down syndrome, I felt overwhelmed, disoriented. I had no idea what it meant. A few days later, while I was still in the hospital, a social worker came in and asked if we wanted to know about adoption. I was shocked.

"What bothers me," she continued, "is that our culture seems to need to have the perfect package at birth. And there's no advocate out there to dispel some of the fears and myths for women who are given this news. My real admiration is for people who know and go ahead. But I also had a very strong sense that things were exactly as they were meant to be, and that I was just catching up."

At my quizzical look, she explained. "When I was pregnant, we went to Maui. Lying on the beach, I said to Harold, 'Look, that family over there, with four kids, their little girl has Down syndrome.' Harold was reading a book, and I don't think he looked up, just did the *hmmm* thing. But then I said, 'I think Down syndrome is something I could handle.'"

Harold walked back into the room and sat down as Leanne said, "Another time, back home, I was having lunch with some girlfriends. I saw a young woman with Down syndrome, and I felt an overwhelming sense of panic. I had no idea why. My friends said, 'Leanne, your baby's fine.'"

Harold took up the story. "In a way, we felt blessed that we didn't know. We would have worried so much."

Leanne nodded. "When Jack was about six months old, I was feeling happy most of the time, except for regular bouts of panic. I knew there were friends and people I'd worked with who felt sorry for us, who just couldn't see us. And I really struggled with that."

"We might have been the same," Harold interjected.

"Finally," Leanne said, "I called a woman I knew who had a son with Down syndrome, and I asked her, 'Is this a big deal?'"

Leanne laughed. "She said no. That helped but it didn't stop my moments of panic. Then one day, I was walking on the seawall with Jack in his buggy, and I just had the thought: This is not a big deal. This is my son. We're going to raise him to be a happy boy."

• • •

KATHLEEN LOVED BEING in Leanne's classroom. When I asked Kathleen what she liked so much, she told me they mostly talked and had fun. I realized that Leanne was one of those rare teachers who could make learning seem effortless, as if it really were all talk and fun. Her class learned about the human digestive system, for example, by performing a play called *Harriet the Hamburger.* Harriet's storyline was simple: she's eaten and passes through to the very end of the digestive system. All the organs along the way had speaking roles in the play. Harriet was doomed, but she dramatized the human digestive system in a way that held a lot of appeal for nine- and ten-year-olds.

Sometime during the spring of that year, as Kathleen and her class began to rehearse *Harriet,* I received a call from my younger brother, David, late one Sunday night. "Hey, Jude," he said, using the name both my brothers had called me since we were small. He sounded exhausted, beaten down. Not the brother I knew, who shouldered most things with a cheerful shrug. Both David and my older brother, John, had been alternating weeks, staying with my parents to help them out. I'd made the trip from Vancouver as often as I could.

"How is she?" I asked, not sure I wanted to hear the details. By now, my mother's oncologist had signed off, telling us that the chemotherapy and radiation treatments that had eased her through the four years since her diagnosis wouldn't help her anymore. David let out a slow breath. "I don't think I can do this anymore. I can't pick her up by myself, and John has to go back to work this week."

I didn't know what to say. I'd just returned home from visiting my parents a week earlier. My husband, Jim, was planning to leave the next day on a trip to the U.S. and our children, all still in elementary school, needed one of us to be with them. We had no handy backup, no nearby family, we could call to step in for us.

"I think we're going to have to take her to the hospital." I heard defeat in David's voice. My mother had been in and out of the hospital many times since her diagnosis. When I'd left her the last time, as I bent close to say goodbye, she'd whispered, "I don't want to go to the hospital ever again." I'd nodded, silently promising her that I would do whatever I could to prevent that from happening.

"I'll be there tomorrow." My words surprised me. I didn't know how Jim would react, how our children would react. When I told Jim I'd be leaving the next day, he looked at me and, in one of those moments that in hindsight define a marriage, said, "Go. She needs you."

When I arrived, David opened the door and wrapped his arms around me, his shoulders shaking. My burly younger brother was crying into my neck. We broke apart at the faint sandpaper sound of my father's slippers and turned as my ninety-year-old father, stooped but still physically fit (he'd skied until he was eighty-five), entered the hallway. He looked at me, his face pleasant but curious, the look he'd give a friendly stranger, then something broke through and he stepped toward me, arms held out.

"Oh, Judy, you're here at last," he said, pulling me into a close hug. "I'm so glad." My undemonstrative father tightened his hug until I couldn't breathe.

"Dad," I gasped.

"Sorry," he said, "it's just that—" His blue eyes locked on mine. The moment stretched out as I waited for him to continue. But as I stood in front of him, our connection vanished, and I reverted to friendly stranger. "Well," he said, "well. Would you like a cup of tea?" And so began a stay that turned into almost two months. I moved into the second bedroom of my parents' condominium, and my brothers took turns staying for a week at a time.

The first night, Kathleen called me after dinner. "Mum?" At eight, Kathleen still liked to tell me everything about her day. "Mum, guess what? I got the lead!" As a child who'd announced at the age of four, after seeing a children's performance of Agatha Christie's *The Mousetrap,* "I want to do that," I knew this was big news for Kathleen. "Great!" I said, mustering the small bit of enthusiasm I could after my long drive.

"Mum. The play we're doing. *Harriet the Hamburger.*"

"You're the hamburger?"

"Yes! And I talk all the way to the end!"

"Really?" I didn't want to imagine what Harriet's last words would be.

"Yeah. And you have to make a puppet to fit on my hand, so Harriet can talk."

"Sweetie," I began. Kathleen knew why I was here, but she didn't like to talk about her grandmother being sick. "I can't do that right now."

Silence. "But, Mom," she tried again, "you have to."

"You're going to have to ask Dad." More silence. "You know, he's pretty good with a glue gun."

Kathleen snorted. "Dad hates stuff like that."

She was right, but I wasn't going to admit that now. "Just ask him, okay?" I listened as Kathleen started to cry. She began softly, like a low static on the line, but quickly escalated to clear sobs, her breath becoming ragged. I tried to talk over it, telling her again that her grandmother needed me, that her father could make a hand puppet, and that friends would help if needed.

"It's not the same," she said. "I want you to do it."

For the next month, Kathleen phoned me almost every night. We had the same conversation, or variations of it, every time—she told me why I was the only one who could make Harriet, and I reminded her why it was impossible for me to do that right now. Sometimes I tried to tell her about her grandmother, but that only made Kathleen cry harder.

And there wasn't much I could say that an eight-year-old could absorb. The words that adults used to ease the pain, like *peaceful* or *sleeping,* seemed false. My mother was sleeping most of the time, but sometimes she gasped awake as her pain spiked out of control. Her young doctor, who was by now stopping every night on her way home from work, had told us to buy some liquid morphine. When a gasp startled us, one of us would get the brown bottle and spoon tiny amounts into my mother's parched mouth. Sometimes it dribbled out of the sides of her mouth, and we tried again and again until we thought she'd swallowed a few drops. She was already on a high dose of morphine pills and her doctor had warned us that soon she'd lose her ability to swallow. I didn't want to think about what happened after that, but I knew using the word *peaceful* was a lie.

IN THE LAST week of my mother's life, Kathleen's phone calls stopped. Jim may have told me that her play took place, but I don't remember. By then, I was moving slowly through the cold air that had settled in my parents' condominium. My brothers and I—by now, it took all three of us to manage—stumbled from moment to moment as our mother retreated further each day from the conscious world. Our father stumbled around, too, often staying in his blue-striped pyjamas for the entire day.

THE LAST NIGHT, my brothers and I sat in our parents' bedroom, David on the floor, leaning against the wall, John on my father's twin bed, and me, perched on the end of my mother's bed. Her breathing had grown deeper and more sporadic throughout the day. By the late afternoon, each breath seemed an immense struggle and the gaps between breaths impossibly long.

My father shuffled back and forth between the bedroom and the kitchen. From the bedroom, we could hear him fill up the electric kettle we'd bought so he wouldn't have to turn on the stove, and between my mother's breaths we heard the kettle come to a boil, water pouring slowly as my father warmed the teapot the way he'd always done. Often he'd call out to us, "Tea anyone?" But today, as the light outside faded, he padded back into the bedroom, a cup in one hand, his eyes red. As he looked at us, his face brightened and he said, "Time for some supper, don't you think?"

John looked up. "I'll order something in," he said. But he didn't move, staring, as we all were, at our mother, a thin, still figure under her blue quilt. "Pizza, maybe," John added, but it was as if he were telling himself and no one else.

My father padded around to my mother, placing his hand on her forehead. "Kate," he said, his voice low. He smoothed a few wisps of still-dark hair back from her forehead. "Katie, it's time to wake up." I glanced at my brothers. David had let his head fall back and was staring at the stippled ceiling. John stood up and stepped toward my father.

"Dad," he said, taking my father's arm, "come sit down."

My father yanked his arm away. "We have to eat. What's she thinking? Supper will just appear?" He twisted up the quilt close to my mother's face.

John grabbed his arm and held him tight. I could see my father's face grow red. I stood up and turned to him.

"Dad," I said, "she's dying." My words felt like a brutal stab, but I didn't know how else to get through to him. He slumped down on the side of his bed and put his head in his hands.

"Oh," he said. "I forgot."

As the night wore on, the time between my mother's breaths grew impossibly long. It was as if we couldn't breathe until we heard her draw another breath. Sometime during the late evening, I bent down close to her, putting my hands on her bony shoulders, my face a few inches from hers. "I love you," I whispered.

I thought I'd left it too late, that it was impossible she could hear me now. But I heard a faint intake of breath, and as she breathed out, a whispered rush of words, "Ilove youIloveyou." I let my forehead rest on hers for a moment, not believing what I'd heard. Then I stood up. My father sat on his bed, his head still down, my brothers on the floor. I couldn't move. My mother took a few more breaths and then silence filled the room, pushing out the air, taking my mother with it.

● ● ●

WHEN I FINALLY returned home, I found Harriet buried in the litter of clothes on Kathleen's floor. I marvelled at what Jim had created—a neatly hinged pantyhose bun, into which I could insert my hand, lolling felt tongues of ketch-up and mustard, and dark eyes framed by permanently sur-prised eyebrows. Maybe he'd thought about Harriet's fate as he drew those.

I picked up Harriet and flapped her open and shut a few

times. I felt like hugging her. She'd been the interruption each night as my brothers and I had tried to muster the energy to face the night and the next day. She'd made us smile—"A real talking hamburger, eh?" John had said one night, "Think Jim's up to that?"

But Harriet had been the connection between Kathleen and me during that terrible time. If we couldn't talk about her grandmother dying, at least we could argue about Harriet. And as time passed, Harriet became a symbol of sorts— of my mother's last days, of my father's struggle to stay connected to a painful reality, of the moments when Kathleen's beseeching calls for me to create a talking hamburger gave my brothers and me a reason to laugh, to remember that life would carry on.

- - -

FRIDAY. GRACE'S WRITING book lies unopened on the table. As I settle into the chair beside her I ask, "Can you show me what you've written this week?"

She flips her notebook open with a flourish. "See, I got a whole bunch of the story written." She turns over at least seven pages of neatly printed story. "And I added a lot of details onto the story."

"You've done a lot this week, Grace."

Grace beams as I scan the first page. Verb tenses hop from present to past with abandon and the point of view of the main character, Cinderella-Grace, still moves unfettered from *she* to *I* and back again.

Grace slides her notebook closer to me. "Read, okay?"

During the winter my real mother is about to died. Then when I turned around and I saw my stepmother looking evil, mean eyes at me. I was crying beside my real mother's bed! The two evil and ugly, mean stepsisters are standing close to their mother. Cinderella's mom's room is very dark, and there's only one lit candle beside the bed!

Partway through Grace edges her chair close to mine, and I feel her head land softly on my shoulder.

Outside there is a real thunder booming loudly, and they hear the voice of God talking to them. The voice of God warns stepmother, "You must leave Cinderella ALONE or else your accountable SOUL will be TAKEN!"

When she looks at the thunder in the sky and her body shakes so hard and she feels a little bit of tense about God. In her deepest heart, she knows that she just overheard the thunder outside and she also heard the voice of God! God is beside her and she is not ALONE.

After several pages, I stop reading. "We have to talk about something, Grace. Something we talked about before. A writing thing."

"What's that?" Grace lifts her head and looks up at me.

"Point of view. Remember we talked about that? How writers call it POV?"

"Oh." Grace looks down. "I forget that."

"That's okay. Everyone forgets things. Even"—I lower my voice, as if confiding a terrible secret—"me."

Grace giggles. "Oh, you always make me laugh."

I point to the sentences I've just read. "You see here how you started your story—'Once upon a time, there is a lady called Cinderella-Grace.' As if you're talking about 'her' or 'she.' But here"—I turn the page—"here you say, 'I was crying beside my real mother's bed!' You're talking about 'I' or 'me.'"

"What do you mean?"

"I mean you can tell your whole story using 'I' instead of 'she.'"

"Oh."

I hesitate. I'd like to add, "You can write your story as if you're Cinderella," but that seems a leap that Grace should make, if anyone does.

"Oh." Grace stares at me, a thoughtful look on her face. "As if it's me?"

I nod. "What do you think?"

"I'm not sure." Grace leans her head against my shoulder again. "Read more, okay?"

- - -

AT THE CORNER, Grace and I wait for the light to change. We're on our way to photocopy the pages Grace has written so far, forty-five in all. Just ahead of us, a mother stands with her small boy, his hand firmly clasped in hers. Grace shifts her backpack and looks up at me with a quick smile. "After this, want to go for a coffee?" As I nod, the small boy twists around and stares up at Grace. His mother glances down at her son, her eyes following his. In that fleeting moment, I see her face harden. When the light changes, she gives her son's arm a sharp tug, as if she can't wait to get away from us.

In *Becoming Human,* Jean Vanier writes: "The social stigmas around people with intellectual disabilities are strong. There is an implicit question: If someone cannot live according to the values of knowledge and power, the values of the greater society, we ask ourselves, can that person be fully human?" In 1964, Vanier had founded L'Arche, an international organization dedicated to providing support for those with intellectual disabilities, to providing the stigmatized with homes.

Is this what I'm seeing today? A look from a well-dressed mother, with her small and still-perfect son, that openly questions whether Grace is human?

Vanier adds, "We are all frightened of the ugly, the dirty. We all want to turn away from anything that reveals the failure, pain, sickness, and death beneath the brightly painted surface of our ordered lives." He maintains that the intellectually disabled "are among the most oppressed and excluded people in the world."

Vanier is not alone in his opinion. Robert Murphy, author of *The Body Silent*, says the disabled subvert our ideal of beauty and virility, and "to the extent that we depart from the ideal, we become ugly and repulsive." The disabled, Murphy writes, "serve as constant, visible reminders to the able-bodied that the society they live in is shot through with inequity and suffering, that they live in a counterfeit paradise, that they too are vulnerable. We represent a fearsome possibility." Murphy speaks with the authority of personal experience: he wrote *The Body Silent* after a spinal tumor forced him to use a wheelchair.

That "fearsome possibility" is brought to life in an unforgettable way in Alice Munro's short story *Child's Play*. Charlene and Marlene, young girls of nine or ten, meet at summer camp. They immediately begin to sort out their similarities—they both have had their tonsils removed—and their differences—both have brown hair, but one was "wavy" and the other "bushy."

They move on to compare family stories, culminating in the most disgusting details of their young lives. Charlene tells of stumbling upon her older brother while he was having sex and seeing his bare "white bum."

Marlene trumps Charlene's story by telling her about Verna, an older neighbourhood girl who isn't able to read, or write, or play games, a girl who has squinting eyes and an oddly small head. The same Verna who's shown up at the summer camp as one of "the Specials."

Marlene recalls that she told her mother when Verna arrived in the neighbourhood that she hated her. And then the adult Marlene elaborates on what that word "hate" can mean to children—that it may mean they are afraid not of some physical danger, but of something more elusive, a kind of "spell or dark intention." And that was what Marlene, as a child, feared about Verna.

Marlene resists her mother's entreaties to be kind to Verna and acknowledges that she dislikes everything about Verna, even her name. When her mother asks her how she can blame someone for the way she was born, Marlene admits that she does blame Verna; that even at her young age, she understands from the way the grown-ups around her react that there was an unspoken agreement that people like Verna were to blame for how they were. And in spite of her mother's efforts to change Marlene's feelings about Verna, Marlene suspects that underneath, her mother feels the same as she does.

Some years later, Marlene receives a letter from Charlene's husband, telling her that her friend is dying. Marlene reluctantly goes to visit Charlene, but she's asleep. A nurse gives Marlene a note in which Charlene asks her to see a priest who "will know what to do," and assures Marlene that it has nothing to do with her. Marlene is unable to find the priest named by her friend. As she leaves the church, she briefly thinks about seeking forgiveness herself, but rejects the idea.

Child's Play ends with Marlene recalling the final day at summer camp—the last swim in the lake before parents arrived to pick up their daughters, the way a couple of motorboats raced too close to the swimmers and set up a wave that swamped Marlene, Charlene, and Verna, who was wading toward them. How the wave pitched Verna forward, and Marlene and Charlene found Verna floating just below the surface of the water, slowly turning, "light as a jellyfish in the water." How they put their hands on her pale blue rubber cap, and held Verna's head under. Marlene says they didn't feel that they were "triumphing in our wickedness," but that they were doing what they were clearly meant to do.

Looking back many years later, Marlene concedes that she and Charlene had gone too far, that there was no turning back at that point. And she recognizes something even more devastating: that it had not occurred to the two young girls that they had a choice in what they were doing, that they could have stopped. That Verna didn't need to die.

Munro is far too subtle to spell it out, but there it is, the recognition in the young girls' act, that slow, repulsive Verna deserved what happened to her. That the girls were only doing what was expected of them.

I read Munro's story with a strange combination of horror and reluctant recognition. Horror that she had taken the story where she had, and recognition that I understood the abhorrence that Charlene and Marlene felt when they saw Verna wading toward them.

I THINK ABOUT the doughnut girl in my small town. Was she as shunned as I think? My memory offers up only a few sparse details—walking along the main street, seeing her with a doughnut on each finger, hearing voices call out to her, "Hey, re-tard!" Were those voices telling her, as I sensed as a young girl, that she had no place in our town?

AND WHY ARE we so afraid of the Vernas of the world? Of the doughnut girls? Of the Graces? What makes them the "fearsome possibility" Robert Murphy describes—the reminder that we live in a world "shot through with inequity and suffering...a counterfeit paradise, that [we] too are vulnerable"?

WHILE A PHD student at Harvard, Martha Beck discovered she was expecting a baby with Down syndrome. Against almost unanimous advice from her university world to have an abortion, she and her husband decided to continue with the pregnancy. After her son's birth, Beck describes how she carried him in a front baby carrier in the first days when she returned to her classes, and no one would look at her baby. If they had to talk to her, they kept their eyes fixed on her face, "as though looking down a few inches at Adam would pull them tumbling into some inescapable abyss."

Expecting Adam is the story of Martha Beck's son and how he changed her. Shortly after his birth, she describes sitting with her "tiny orange son" and feeling terror that he would destroy her carefully constructed façade as an intelligent, high-achieving human being. She realized that the labels that could be applied to her son"—that he was "stupid, ugly, strange, clumsy, slow, inept"—could just as easily be applied to her from time to time. It was as if tiny Adam was tangible evidence of her own flaws and vulnerability, physical proof that she was not the perfect Martha she had tried so hard to be. Is that it then? That we fear that we could become, or we could produce, or perhaps most terrifying of all, that we already carry the seeds of being as defective as the person we see in front of us? Is that what makes us turn away, shun, even kill?

And how does this relate to me? Am I afraid that like Grace, I'll be seen as someone who can never be a writer?

And worse, that I'm as invisible as she seems to be?

IN THE PHOTOCOPY shop, Grace pulls her writing out of her backpack. Behind the counter is a young woman who's a recent graduate from the same high school my children attended. Through my frequent visits to this shop, I've learned that like Grace, she's an immigrant. A few weeks earlier, she'd told me that the year before, she'd lost her two best friends, fellow Iranian immigrants, when they skied into an out-of-bounds area on a local ski hill and got lost. Their bodies were found in a deep, snow-choked gully. "It was their first time skiing, ever," she'd told me, her usually cheerful face pale.

Now she smiles at me. "Hi. What have you got today?"

Graces flops her stack of papers on the counter. "All these."

The young woman looks uncertainly from me to Grace and back to me.

"Grace is writing a book," I explain, "and we need to copy the pages so we can edit them more easily."

She smiles as she looks at Grace. "Really. Wow. A book." She picks up the stack of papers. "One copy?"

"Yes," Grace nods, following closely as the young woman walks to one of the copying machines.

As the papers begin to feed through the machine and spit out the other side, Grace crouches down on her knees, her face close to the growing stack of copies. "Amazing," she breathes, as if she'd like to inhale her story, one page at a time.

PART THREE

My Real Truth

ON A BLUSTERY November day, Kathleen and I sat in a steamy coffee shop in the East Village of Manhattan. In her final year of high school, Kathleen was here to audition for the highly competitive theatre program at New York University. Ever since her first taste of drama playing Harriet the Hamburger in elementary school, Kathleen had been bitten by the thespian bug. This audition was, I realized, the culmination of every class, every audition, every performance she'd ever taken part in. Now, hunched over the faux marble top of our small table, she wanted to go over, and over and over, her monologues for her audition that afternoon. One comedic, the other dramatic, they were meant to show her acting chops in two-minute bursts.

"I want to talk to you about life," Kathleen began, staring at me. Her hair pulled back in a tight ponytail, dark circles under her eyes, I sensed the strain she was feeling. I knew that she thought this was her one shot at training in one of the theatre capitals of the English-speaking world. I'd suggested other possibilities, not wanting her to count so heavily on something that seemed like such a long shot. But she'd never wavered in her focus. This was where she wanted to be. And although I wouldn't have admitted it as we sat at that table, I also knew that something else was driving me to extraordinary lengths to support her over-the-moon dream. My failure at her age to follow my own dream.

FROM HER YEARS in school and community plays, I'd learned that eye contact while I listened to Kathleen's lines was a bad thing. Her eyes were free to go wherever they needed to go, but mine were supposed to hang onto some spot on the wall, never connecting with hers, at the same time seeing every subtle twist of her mouth, every lift of an eyebrow. I found a spot in the coffee shop just above her head and did my best to see but not look. Kathleen continued with Woman's opening speech from *Laughing Wild*, Christopher Durang's play about a woman just released from a mental institution: "It's just too difficult to be alive, isn't it, and to try to function?"

This was the comedic monologue. For the dramatic one, she'd chosen a speech from the conclusion of *'night, Mother*, Marsha Norman's Pulitzer Prize–winning and devastating play about an epileptic woman who wants to kill herself, and her mother's desperate and ultimately unsuccessful attempt to stop her.

We sat in the coffee shop for almost two hours, ignoring the stocky busboy who swept past several times, wanting to clear our table. Finally, we shrugged on our coats and left. A heavy rain fell, but in the crawling traffic, walking would be faster than taking a taxi to the studio where the auditions would be held.

At the corner, huddled under our shared umbrella, Kathleen continued with Woman's speech: "I tried to buy a can of tuna fish in the supermarket, and there was this person standing right in front of where I wanted to reach out to get the tuna fish, and I waited a while, to see if they'd move, and they didn't—they were looking at tuna fish too, but they were taking a long time on it…" The light changed and we started across the street. At the curb, a wide puddle blocked us. The umbrella and I went one way, Kathleen the other. As water streamed down her face, she shouted: "…and this stupid person didn't grasp that I needed to get by them to get the goddam tuna fish, people are so insensitive, I just hate them, and so I reached over with my fist, and I brought it down real hard on his head and I screamed: 'Would you kindly move, asshole!!'" Not a single head turned.

Fifteen more blocks to go. As we trudged on through the rain, Kathleen switched to her dramatic monologue. "I am what became of your child," she began. With every repetition of this line, heads turned. Eyes fixed on me and I saw the assumption—so you're one of those monster mothers who drive their daughters over the edge.

"Try saying it more softly," I suggested.

At the studio, we entered a big room filled with a palpable nervous energy as students, most with parents beside them, sweated out the wait for their turn for the ten-minute interview. A father in the row just ahead of us leaned forward, head in his hand, as if he'd already had bad news. His son sat bolt upright beside him, mouthing his lines, one knee jackknifing up and down. Other students repeated their lines, some silently, others in loud, I-don't-care-who-hears-me voices. One boy, garish scarf hanging almost to his knees, stalked around the edge of the room gesturing wildly as he mumbled his lines.

Beside me, Kathleen recited her lines in a low voice. After a few minutes, she turned to me. "I have to say them to you, okay?" She worked through Woman's tuna fish speech without any major hitches. But as she began Jessie's monologue from Marsha Norman's *'night, Mother,* she hesitated. "I am what became of your child," she said, staring into my eyes. Here there was no easy wall, no spot where my eyes could retreat into non-contact. I stared back, held by the intensity of her gaze. Kathleen continued, her voice slowing. "I found an old baby picture of me. And it was somebody else, not me. It was somebody pink and fat who never heard of sick or lonely..." With each word, Kathleen seemed to fall deeper into Jessie's character, a woman in her late thirties who'd lived with uncontrollable epilepsy for most of her life. I couldn't look away, couldn't think of anything except the words Kathleen was saying.

As I listened, I became Jessie's mother hearing my daughter tell me why she was going to kill herself that very night: "So, see, it doesn't much matter what else happens in the world or in this house, even. I'm what was worth waiting for and I didn't make it. Me...who might have made a difference to me...I'm not going to show up, so there's no reason to stay, except to keep you company, and that's...not reason enough because I'm not...very good company. (A pause) Am I."

As Kathleen finished, tears rolled down my face. I swiped them away with the back of my hand, conscious that those around me must be thinking that here was the supposedly supportive parent, losing it. Kathleen sat for a moment and then threw her arm around my shoulder. "It's okay, Mum," she said with a small laugh. "Like you always say, it's not real." But her face was as drawn as mine, and I knew she had entered Jessie's mind and had understood why she was giving up on herself.

A few minutes later, Kathleen's name was called, and she disappeared down the hallway. As I stared ahead, still overcome with my reaction to her monologue, a hand tapped me on the shoulder from behind. Turning back, I saw the worried face of another mother. "Oh my," she said, "the stress is really getting to you and your daughter, isn't it?"

WHEN WE FLEW home after Kathleen's audition, I thought I should try to help her prepare for the most likely result of her audition. Rejection. "You know," I began somewhere over what I thought was Manitoba, a flat expanse winking with dozens of small lakes, "they have hundreds of applicants." Kathleen jerked her head up from her magazine. "And they reject most of them." I'd thought of saying nothing, of waiting for the letter to arrive. But she was aiming for something where the odds of success were very low.

For a moment, I remembered Grace in my dark car, singing "Impossible," as if an invisible audience were asking her to sing it again and again. In a way, the audience for Kathleen seemed almost as invisible.

Kathleen stared back at me. "I'm going to believe," she finally said, dropping her eyes to her magazine.

I leaned back in my seat, unable to say anything. She hasn't heard that cold hiss I heard at her age—*What makes you think you can do anything?*

I'm going to believe. I savoured her words, tasting the strange, bright hope of them.

●●●

IN HIGH SCHOOL, Grace had a full-time teaching assistant. She took part in regular art, physical education, cooking, sewing, and some social studies and science classes. For her other subjects, she attended simplified classes. But high school became a lonely place. Although Grace had friends in elementary school, Jessica tells me, she had only one good friend in high school, Samara.

Samara Gossen, now twenty-six and living on Vancouver Island, the mother of two young daughters, tells me how she met Grace. "It was a grade eight or nine physical education class. Grace didn't seem unhappy, and no one made fun of her, but no one paid any attention to her either. So

I decided she needed to be with someone. To have a friend, like anyone else."

"We started hanging out in that class together," Samara continues. "I'm not sure, Grace might have invited me to have lunch with her in the special education room. Anyway," she laughs, "we started having lunch together most days."

Eventually, Samara met Jessica, who invited her to visit Grace at home. "When I went to see Grace, we'd play board games, like Monopoly and Life." She laughs again. "Grace loved Monopoly. She always had her calculator with her, so she could figure out the money."

As Samara tells me about her friendship with Grace, I'm struck by how rare it is for this to happen. I ask her why she did what no one else had done.

"When I see other people not having a good time, I try to include them," she says.

"But why?" I ask, pressing her. "When so many people just don't know how to approach someone like Grace, or are uneasy, why did you do this? What made you realize Grace needed a friend?"

It takes a moment for Samara to answer. "When I was in elementary school," she finally says, "I was severely bullied. There was one girl, she coordinated a bunch of practical jokes on me. Kids would steal my jacket, put stuff in my desk. They even put some bees in my desk one day!" She stops. "Finally, my family moved so I could go to a different school."

Samara's ordeal, one you'd never wish on any young child, or anyone at any age, has clearly had an impact on how she sees someone like Grace. Is it because she was once forced into the role of the "other" that she is able to see and understand, more than the rest of us, what that role feels like? Did that experience let her see what others couldn't, or wouldn't see? That a slight girl in a gym class, someone mildly different, with a shy smile, was lonely and wanted a friend?

●●●

GRACE'S HIGH SCHOOL experience highlighted the difference, often gaping, between official "inclusion" and real belonging. But by the time she started high school, the fight parents had waged for inclusion of their children in regular schools was considered over. So what was it like before inclusion was accepted? Who were the students who'd fought to attend a regular school?

I meet Russell Morfitt at Thrifty's in Victoria. Russell has worked there part-time for over ten years. For most of that time, his job has been to "face" the milk, to stand at the back of the cold dairy case for several hours each day and turn the milk cartons and jugs so their labels face out to customers. On his breaks in the warmth of the store, he helps out with other displays, or, as his manager, a young man not much older than Russell, says when I meet him, "Anything I think needs to be done." A quick smile softens his words as he adds, "And Russ never lets me down." Russell, wearing a green Thrifty's apron with a white name tag pinned to it, beams.

Recently, Russell has been promoted to handling eggs. He checks for broken eggs and arranges the cartons in the display case. His mother, Peggy, tells me Russell has "soared since the eggs." When I first see Russell, he's in the lineup at one of the tills, waiting to pay for a few things at the end of his shift. It's the late-afternoon witching hour, when the lines at the tills begin to stretch out and impatience builds as blood sugar drops.

At till number four, the lineup has ground to a halt and signs of impatience are flaring up. A mother snaps at her toddler *stop, now;* a white-haired man rests his elbows on the handle of his mostly empty cart, a stoic look on his face.

The young man holding up till number four is Russell. Just over five feet tall, stocky, with his brown hair gelled up in the front, and an open, friendly face, Russell, thirty-one, punches his pin into the debit machine with a stubby forefinger. It doesn't work. Peggy, standing beside me at the end of the checkout counter, mutters, "Numbers are a problem." Her son doesn't give up, punches the keypad again. The cashier, a girl who looks like she's barely in high school, glances at the line and gives Russell a quick smile. Her polite way, I see, of telling him to hurry up. Peggy walks to her son.

"Russell," she says, "look at me." She holds up her fingers to signal each number, waiting as Russell punches it in and looks up at her again, ready for the next one.

In a moment, a quick buzz signals that Russell has successfully accessed his account, and the cashier slips Russell's receipt into his bag of groceries. "See ya, Russ," she says, with a quick wave. "Here tomorrow?"

Russell wraps a strong arm around his bag and pulls it into his chest. "Yeah, see you tomorrow."

Russell owns his own condominium, pays his own mortgage, and is engaged to be married. "Not for the first time, either," his mother confides. He loves sports, belonging to Special Olympics, where he takes part in track, golf, bowling, and softball. Details that lead you to think he's a regular young guy. And he is, in so many ways.

When I meet Russell for coffee at the end of his shift, I tell him I'm writing a book about working with Grace on her book. "It'll partly be about what it's like to have Down syndrome," I add.

He leans across the table toward me, agitated. "Don't," he says. He wants to say more, but his mouth isn't co-operating. He fixes me with an intense look. Finally, he says, "Don't say Down." Russ's intense reaction to the word *Down,* the same reaction I've encountered in Grace, surprises me.

Peggy fills in the details that help me understand her son's reaction. When Russell was just beginning his education, Peggy wanted to send him to a regular preschool. The nearby special needs preschool, she felt, didn't provide positive role modelling for her son. So Peggy enrolled Russell in a parent participation preschool, where he thrived.

"When it was time for him to go to elementary school," Peggy says, "he thought he'd go to the same school his older brother and sisters attended." She smiles. "The school board had other ideas. It thought Russell should go to a separate school for kids like him." Russell wasn't happy, she says, insisting that he wanted to follow his siblings.

"So," says Peggy, "I sat him down when he was five and told him what he had to do in the interview with the director of special education. Be on his very best behaviour. Not talk unless someone spoke to him." She smiles again. "I was asking him, a five-year-old boy with Down syndrome, to be a model child. I didn't really have high hopes we'd succeed, but I was going to make sure we gave it our best shot."

In wanting to follow his sisters and brother to school, Russell was bumping up against the accepted policy of the day. Children with mental disabilities were sent to separate schools.

And there was no law that Peggy could fall back on to force the school board to accept her son in a regular school.

It was a different story in the United States. In 1954, the landmark case of *Brown v. Board of Education of Topeka* established that "separate educational facilities are inherently unequal." That case was brought by thirteen black parents who had tried to register their children in white schools but had been rejected. The Brown decision was used by parents of disabled children to seek the same kind of declaration for their children. And by the 1970s, they'd succeeded: laws that denied equal education to the disabled were declared unconstitutional.

In 1975, the U.S. Congress passed the Education for All Handicapped Children Act (now the Individuals with Disabilities Education Act, or IDEA), which tied federal funding to compliance with the law: a school board had to identify "handicapped" children and provide a free education appropriate to the needs of the specific child, in the "least restrictive environment," a phrase that came to mean inclusion in regular classrooms if at all possible.

No such sweeping legal change occurred in Canada, in part, because education is a provincial matter under the Canadian constitution, and because Canadian courts have been loath to upset decisions made by local school boards and officials.

In 1985, the parents of eight-year-old Aaron Bales, a boy described in court documents as having the mental age of four, used the new Canadian Charter of Rights and Freedoms to argue that by moving their son to a segregated school, the school board was denying him his constitutional right to life, liberty, and security of the person. The B.C. Supreme Court disagreed, saying that while the school board was required to provide a sufficient education for their son Aaron, it was not obligated to integrate him into a regular classroom.

Not long after the *Bales* case, a new section of the Charter of Rights came into force—Section 15, which declared that every individual is equal before the law, without discrimination based on, among other things, mental or physical disability. This section was the legal handle on which parents of disabled children could hang their argument. In B.C., strong lobbying by parents convinced the government to pass in 1989 the Special Needs Students Order. It said:

> A board must provide a student with special needs with an educational program in a classroom where that student is integrated with other students who do not have special needs, unless ... the educational program for the students with special needs should be provided otherwise.

This was the language of inclusion sought by so many parents, but it wasn't there when Peggy needed it. A couple of weeks before the start of elementary school, she and Russell met with the director of special education for their school district. Peggy chuckles. "I couldn't believe it. Russell sat quietly on a chair and said nothing. Until he politely asked if he could write something on the blackboard. He got up, found a piece of chalk, and wrote a perfect letter A. Then he sat down." Her voice echoes the amazement she felt at that moment. "I'll never know whether that's what made them decide to accept Russell, but they did." She laughs. "We couldn't have orchestrated it better if we'd tried."

That victory, sweet as it was, was short-lived. As the end of the kindergarten year approached, Peggy learned that neither grade one teacher wanted Russ in her class. Peggy went to bat for her son again, this time with the support of his kindergarten teacher, persuading the school board that with the aide he'd had in kindergarten, he could manage in a regular classroom.

When Russell was in the middle of grade five, the family moved to Victoria. Peggy discovered that in Victoria there'd been only one student with Down syndrome in the regular school system, a girl. But Peggy was determined. "I just took the attitude," she says, "that Russell's been in regular school so far, and here we are folks!"

Peggy and Russell had to go through another interview, this time with the Victoria superintendent of schools. "Russell," Peggy adds, "was very relaxed this time, sitting back and putting his feet up on the coffee table. I could have killed him!" But she recalls that the superintendent seemed taken with Russell and told her that if she picked the school, he would make it work for Russell.

"It wasn't easy," Peggy says. "The school we went to had never had anyone like Russell before." But he learned to fit in, figuring out, with Peggy's help, what he needed to know to function in his new school.

In grade eight, Russell joined the boys for industrial education, entering a room filled with power tools, pieces of equipment that demanded all students follow strict safety rules. "The teacher took one look at Russell and told him he couldn't operate any of the equipment," Peggy says. "Russell walked out into the hall and lay down on the floor. The teacher called the principal, and when he arrived, Russell looked up at him from the floor. 'Just walk right on me,' he said. 'That's what you're doing.'"

Russell's protest worked. He stayed in the class and at the end of the term, Peggy says, "that teacher told me he'd had the steepest learning curve he'd ever had with any student, but he learned an immense amount from Russell."

As Russell continued through high school, a question loomed: Would he graduate? No one like Russell had ever written the provincial exams. But he wanted to try. So he wrote the English 12 exam with assistance from a reader and a scribe, receiving a mark of 22 percent. Peggy asked him if he wanted to try again, but he said he was done with exams. He received a modified graduation diploma.

Russell's fight to follow his brother and sisters in regular school tells only part of the story. Inclusion has many variations, from being "mainstreamed" into a regular classroom, to being segregated in a special needs classroom with other special needs students, to some combination of regular and segregated classes, as Grace experienced. It can mean, as many parents have discovered, that physical inclusion—being in the same building as students without special needs—is no guarantee of social inclusion. Of belonging. And it can mean that the special needs student is exposed to ridicule or bullying in a regular school that might be less likely to occur in a segregated environment with other special needs students.

Many parents, however, are willing to take that risk, if it means their child has a chance to find inclusion at a regular school and the possible benefits of friendship and social learning.

In 1995, after Russ had graduated, the Supreme Court of Canada considered the case of Emily Eaton, a twelve-year-old with cerebral palsy. She had vision problems and difficulties communicating, and was in a wheelchair. A tribunal appointed by her local school board decided she would be better off in a partially segregated environment. Her parents objected and appealed. The Ontario Court of Appeal found that Section 15 of the Charter created a presumption in favour of integrating special needs students into regular classrooms. The Brant Board of Education appealed and took the case to the Supreme Court of Canada. To the disappointment of many parents of disabled children, the court said that there was no legal presumption favouring integration in regular classrooms. Instead, the question was whether the tribunal had acted in the best interests of the child, and in this case, the court decided, it had.

But in 2012, another Supreme Court of Canada decision changed the landscape again. As a young student in North Vancouver, B.C., Jeffrey Moore was referred to his local school board's diagnostic centre for help with his severe dyslexia. But the centre closed down because of financial restraints, and the help Jeffrey needed was not available through the public school system. On the recommendation of a school psychologist, Jeffrey's parents sent him to a private school. His father filed a complaint under B.C.'s Human Rights Code, arguing that because his son had been denied a "service customarily available to the public," he'd been discriminated against. The school board, citing severe funding difficulties, argued that Jeffrey's case should be compared to what services had been available to other "special needs" students. On that basis, he'd fared no worse than other students like him.

The Supreme Court of Canada dismissed the school board's argument in a few blunt sentences:

> To define "special education" as the service at issue risks descending into the kind of "separate but equal" approach which was majestically discarded in *Brown v. Board of Education of Topeka,* 347 U.S. 483 (1954). Comparing Jeffrey only with other special needs students would mean the District could cut all special needs programs and yet be immune from a claim of discrimination.

Special education, the court said, is not a luxury, but the means by which children like Jeffrey receive their education.

Jeffrey Moore graduated from a private high school, attended post-secondary education, and now works full-time as a plumber. He sees his legal victory in very personal terms. "I had no idea why everyone in class was moving forward and I was on the sidelines." Now, he says, "Kids are going to get the help they need before the damage is done; before they feel stupid or that they are unable to do anything."

WHEN RUSSELL STARTED preschool, he tried as much as possible to fit in with the other children. One day, as his class played in the playground just outside the preschool, Russell climbed to the top of the monkey bars. A parent, alarmed at what she thought was a dangerous situation, asked if Russell belonged up there. Peggy says she will never forget what Russell's teacher said to the concerned parent: "If Russell made it up there, he belongs there."

■ ■ ■

BY NOW A series of small rituals has developed on my arrival at Grace's house on Friday afternoons. I lift my hand to knock, and the door opens before I knock, just as it did that first day. Jessica smiles and bows as I step inside, slip off my shoes, and slide on the pink chenille slippers that sit neatly beside the door. As Jessica and I chat, Grace appears in the archway that opens to the living and dining rooms.

"Hi, Grace."

She flashes me her quicksilver smile. "Hi, how's it going?"

As we walk to the dining room, I see a computer sitting

at one end of the table. Beside it, Grace's pens, pencils, and notebooks, in their usual precise rows.

Grace pats the top of the computer. "Albert put it all in here!" Her younger brother, Albert, is a computer science major at the University of B.C.

"All your writing?"

"Yes! It's my document file."

Grace sits down. "At Vancouver Community College I took computer classes. Twice."

"That's great that your writing is on your computer now. It'll make editing a lot easier," I say, sitting down beside Grace. "How was your week?"

"Okay."

"Just okay?"

Grace giggles. "I have a date!"

"Who's your date?"

Grace runs her tongue over her lower lip. "My date is Ronald. My boyfriend."

Early in our meetings, Grace had told me about Ronald, a man she'd met in one of her summer school classes who also has Down syndrome. My boyfriend, she said sometimes, and other times, my prince. "I meet him sometimes at the library," she'd told me. "We have coffee and talk."

"We're meeting at the library. For lunch. Next week." Grace giggles again, staring at the screen as she clicks her mouse. The wavy lines that underline spelling or grammatical mistakes are red flags to Grace. As we talk, she hunts them down, clicking them away.

"That sounds like fun."

"Yeah, it will be a lot of fun."

I decide to ask the question I've wanted to ask for a few weeks. "Does Ronald know about your book?"

Grace glances up at me, startled, and then turns back to

the screen. "I don't know."

"Have you told him you're writing a book with a Prince Ronald in it?"

"Not really."

Grace's reticence, her sudden shyness, tells me that her relationship with Ronald is possibly more tentative, or more fictitious, than I'd realized. "Do you think you might want to tell him about it sometime?"

Grace looks at me for a long moment. "Maybe," she says softly.

LAST WEEK, WE'D gone over the chapter where Cinderella-Grace and Prince Ronald get married. Grace had described the wedding in the simplest way:

Prince Ronald and I say "I do" to each other and the minister asks Prince Ronald to kiss me on my red rose gloss lips. We turn around holding our hands together and we wave to everyone!

After a "grand party filled with dancing," the magical night ends: Prince Ronald and I come running through to the grand hall way and down the stairs, where we stop and throw our white wedding flowers together, our hands swinging and flying up high, tossing them over our heads!

When I'd been about to leave that day, I'd asked Grace what she was going to work on next.

"They go on their honeymoon!" she'd said, beaming. "I started it already."

Slipping on my shoes, I'd balanced myself, one hand on the wall. "On the *Titanic?*"

Grace had smiled broadly. "Oh yeah!" On the first day we'd met, Grace had let me know that she knew what had happened to the *Titanic*. Of course. Duh.

"Well," I'd said, "I'll be interested to see how you handle that."

"Okay." Grace had given me a small wave as I'd opened the door. "See ya."

TODAY, I PULL a magazine out of my bag. "Take a look at this, Grace."

It's a *Canadian Geographic* issue featuring an article entitled "Breaking the Ice" by Wayne Curtis. We flip through the pages, marvelling at the full-page photos of glistening blue-white mountains, drifting along Iceberg Alley, the ice-clogged waters off the southeast coast of Newfoundland. Together we read that of the thousands of icebergs that calve off Greenland's glaciers each year, between four hundred and eight hundred drift as far south as Newfoundland. As they float south, they begin to melt and split apart, making it hard for them to be located even by modern-day radar.

Grace studies the map of collisions between icebergs and ships, dozens of small x's forming a circular shadow around the Grand Banks. "So many, I can't count," she breathes. She turns to me. "Why don't they just shoot them?"

I smile, but as we turn the page, there, spelled out in the ice-blue letters of a photo caption is the answer to Grace's question: "In 1959, the U.S. Coast Guard pummeled an iceberg with 3,600 kilograms of bombs in an effort to fragment it. The end result? The iceberg tilted slightly."

"Maybe they should try harder," Grace muses.

WE TURN BACK to Grace's writing from the past week. She's described the young couple arriving at the ship docks, where Prince Ronald points out the *Titanic* to his new bride. *Oh my God*, Cinderella-Grace exclaims, no doubt as some of the real passengers had done, *that is a great big ship!* For a few days, Cinderella-Grace and her Prince have a wonderful time, with a royal dance each night *after the yellow golden sunset disappears in the night!*

Grace has written up to the moment of the crash: *Later one night after midnight, Prince Ronald and I hear the sound of the dark* Titanic *ship crashing into a gigantic iceberg in the dark ice cold sea.*

"So what happens next?" I ask. "How will you make it off the ship?"

Grace looks at me for a moment before answering. "Prince Ronald uses his cellphone to call the royal helicopter."

"And the helicopter arrives in time?"

Grace nods. "It's up in the sky, above the ship."

I sense that Grace is moving into the moment, in her imagination. "Can you write that now?"

She looks at me, then lifts her arms above the table. "Something is swinging down ... it's ... " Her arms sway back and forth.

"A rope?"

"That's it! But it has steps ... "

"A rope ladder?"

"Yes! Prince Ronald climbs up into the helicopter, then he looks down at me." Her face upturned, Grace's hands sway again above the table. "It swings down," she says, "close to my face, but I can't grab it. The ship is moving too much."

"Write that, Grace," I urge. "Just like you see it."

Grace begins to type, hunched forward, her face intense.

I realize, watching her, that Grace has entered the magical place every writer dreams about: the imagined reality of her story. The place where you leave the room you're in and arrive without warning in the place your words have created. Grace's hands, her upturned face, tell me she's on the deck of the *Titanic,* a helicopter hovering above her, the bristly rope ladder swinging tantalizingly close to her outstretched hands, then pulling away.

"How do you feel?" I ask.

"I'm scared!" she whispers. "It's so cold and dark and the helicopter's so loud." Her words pull me in and it's as if I can hear the heavy *thwup-thwup-thwup* of the helicopter over the shouts and cries of the panicking passengers.

"What happens?"

"Prince Ronald looks down at me from the helicopter."

"Write what you see, Grace."

Grace looks at me, her face anxious. "I'm scared."

"Write," I say. "Before it disappears."

Grace turns back to her computer and begins to type as I read over her shoulder.

I shout to my husband, Prince Ronald, "I can't do this!" and my body starts to shake.

Again her words pull me into the scene. It's as if I can feel the icy spray whip up, desperate passengers crowding around us, the black water gleaming in the moonlight.

Prince Ronald yells at me. "Don't look down. I'm right here up high in the helicopter! Don't be afraid, just look straight up high into my eyes. I think you can do it!" Grace's hands rest on her keyboard as she stares at her words.

"What happens?" I whisper.

Hunched forward, Grace types. *All of us are rescued by the royal helicopter, flown away from the* Titanic *ship, and we are safe and sound. We fly on our way to Beverly Hills!* Grace leans back in her chair, her shoulders relaxing.

"Beverly Hills! Why there?"

"I always want to go there." Grace giggles. "See the movie stars! Let's go sometime!"

JESSICA BRINGS IN a small thermos of tea. It's the oolong tea that Grace's father David brings back from Taiwan, a slightly astringent tea that at first seemed too bitter to me, but now I welcome. I pop up the thermos spout and pour a cup of tea. "Good writing today, Grace."

She nods and takes a noisy sip from her glass of juice. "I'm going to a real ball!"

"A ball! Where's it going to be?"

"It's—" Grace hesitates. "Mom! Mom!"

Jessica enters from the kitchen, wiping her hands on her apron.

"Mom, where's the ball?"

Jessica smiles at me. "Oh, that is a dinner and dance, a fundraiser, put on by the Down Syndrome Research Foundation."

Grace exhales noisily. "Don't!" she barks. "Don't say that!"

"Will Ronald be there?" I slip in my question, hoping to divert Grace's attention.

"Yes." She beams. "We will go together, me and my prince." Grace bubbles with her plans. "I'm going to wear my Titanic dress, and get my hair done up." She lifts a strand of her long, dark hair and winds it up over her head.

"You'll be beautiful," I say.

"Yes." Grace lets her hair fall and smiles at me. "I will."

■ ■ ■

FRIDAY AFTERNOON. AFTER the near fiasco of their honeymoon on the *Titanic,* I'm curious to find out what's happened this week to Cinderella-Grace and Prince Ronald. As Grace brings up her latest chapter on her computer, I see there's been a big development:

Prince Ronald sees my face turning like a red rose and that means there's something wrong with my stomach.

Prince Ronald asks me what's wrong and I say, "I . . . I can't breathe, steady, okay, my dear! I need to sit down, all right?" I say, as I puff a little.

Before Prince Ronald can use the emergency phone, I tell him, "I have real human babies inside my body. That's why I can't breathe through my nose."

Prince Ronald calls the ambulance to the international airport! We go straight to the hospital.

At the hospital, the wide main automatic door opens and Prince Ronald runs beside the roller emergency bed with me. "You're going to be fine, my love. You don't need to worry about me, I will be fine," says Prince Ronald.

The doctor gives the three babies girls to me and I hug my babies.

I turn to Grace. "So Cinderella-Grace is a mom now?"

"Yes."

"Do her babies have names?"

"Not yet." Grace glances up at me. "I'm going to pick the names soon."

"And how does Cinderella-Grace feel?"

"She's okay. But the babies wake up at night and cry. Jeez! She's really tired."

"Is she happy even though she's tired?"

Grace stares at me for a moment. "I don't know. It's hard to have babies."

I nod again. Memories of our three children, born within a span of four years, flood back. "You're right. It's a lot of hard work. Exhausting."

"Yeah," says Grace. "I know."

●●●

FRIDAY AFTERNOON. I arrive to discover that during the past week, Grace has found both names and precise measurements for Cinderella-Grace's babies:

Morrison, the first born, black hair, yellow eyes, height 12 inches, weight 5 pounds,

Veronica, the second born, blonde, blue eyes, height 11.1 inches, weight 6 pounds,

Mandy, the third born, orange hair, green eyes, height 11.0 inches, weight 7 pounds.

"Do you like them?" Grace asks. I nod and start to read what Grace has written the past week.

What do you think, my dear sweetheart? Cinderella-Grace asks her prince. Prince Ronald smiles. *I like those names.*

And with that, *the nurse hands the three babies to us, and… we all get into the royal long black limousine, and we are on our way to the white castle!*

Cinderella-Grace and Prince Ronald are now international spies and their three daughters, mere babies the previous week, have also begun to train to become "serious international spies … to save the whole world."

As we go over what Grace has written, she flips up the bottom of her T-shirt to scratch around a small white square of gauze. "Itchy," she says, her eyes on her screen as she zaps the red and green wavy lines that flag spelling and grammar mistakes.

LATER, JESSICA EXPLAINS. "Grace has some surgery. So she cannot get pregnant. She understands she cannot look after a baby, and she agrees, this is the best thing to do."

That's when I make the connection. That not long after the time Grace and Jessica must have been talking about the procedure, Grace gave her fictional Cinderella-Grace what she would never have.

•••

STERILIZATION. I KNEW it was a loaded word when applied to the intellectually challenged, one that carried a heavy weight of history. But how had that history played out? How was it that we once thought that sterilizing the intellectually challenged, without their consent, was the right thing to do?

As Michael Bérubé, a professor of literature and the Director of the Institute for the Arts and Humanities at Penn State University, whose son Jamie has Down syndrome, asks in his book, *Life As We Know It*, how can we tell the story of (in his words) "mental retardation?" And how, in telling that story, can we understand the present for "mentally retarded" children and adults?

How can I understand Grace's present unless I understand the past of earlier Graces?

DAVID WRIGHT, IN *Downs: The History of a Disability*, begins in the thirteenth century, when an early English statute drew a clear line between idiocy, a permanent condition from birth, and lunacy, a potentially temporary condition that could include periods of lucidity. The distinction had important legal consequences: the king could hold and manage an idiot's land until his death, when it reverted to his heirs, while a lunatic's lands could only be held until he regained his sanity.

And who was considered an "idiot"? Henry Swinburne, an English lawyer, in *A Briefe Treatise of Testaments and Last Willes* (1590), came up with the definition that would be used for a couple of centuries: "An idiote, or a natural fool is he, who notwithstanding he bee of lawful age, yet he is so witlesse, that he cannot number to twentie, nor can he tell what age he is of, nor knoweth who is his father."

A test that would clearly exclude Grace.

By the eighteenth century, juries of "respectable men" were holding public enquiries (called, interestingly, inquisitions) to determine if someone was a lunatic or idiot, how mentally impaired he was, and what was to be done about him and his property.

The destitute idiot was a different problem. He fell under the Poor Laws, which made church parishes responsible for feeding and housing the poor, often by contracting family or neighbours to care for them. Although the mistreated "village idiot" has a permanent place in literature, Wright points out that there are few documented cases of poor idiot children being abandoned to roam the streets.

The medical community had little interest in idiocy, considering it a permanent condition about which nothing could be done. But fundamental changes in how human beings were seen would lead to changes in medical attitudes.

In the seventeenth century, John Locke had argued that humans are born with a blank mind, a tabula rasa, not with innate ideas and morals as earlier philosophers and theologians believed. Knowledge, Locke said, came from our senses and our thoughts. And idiots, with their lack of reasoning and ideas, proved his point—they, more than anyone, lacked innate ideas. Locke's writings fuelled the growing view that the human mind—any human mind—could be improved, given the right circumstances.

And it was this thought that spiked medical interest in the disabled. They became guinea pigs in experiments designed to test whether education and training could improve their lot, thus proving that our human experience was what defined us, not innate ideas and morals.

Schools and institutes to study blind, deaf, and mute children sprang up all over Europe. This initiative led to similar questions about idiot children. In France, medical men like Jean Itard and Édouard Séguin began working with idiot children, hoping to establish that they too could benefit from training and education. In 1850, Séguin emigrated to the U.S., where he worked in one of the earliest asylums for "feeble-minded" children. He believed that the "feeble-minded" could, through training and socialization, learn to become useful members of society, an idea that was taking hold not only in the U.S. but across western Europe.

Support for separate asylums for the deaf, the blind, the epileptic, and the idiot, places distinct from asylums for lunatics, began to build. Idiot children did not belong with insane and possibly violent adults in lunatic asylums. Supporters cited disturbing examples to gain support for new separate institutions. Dorothea Dix, an American reformer, wrote of "one idiot subject chained, and one in a close stall for seventeen years … [and] three idiots. Never removed from one room."

In England, John Conolly led the fight for separate institutions for idiot children. In 1847, he joined forces with Andrew Reed, a Congregationalist minister, and together they raised the funds to build the large institution that became the Royal Earlswood Asylum for Idiots—the place where a young John Langdon Down would begin his work and, as David Wright has written, would "forever change the history of Down's syndrome."

So how did we go from the relatively enlightened view that "idiot" children could be educated, trained, and become useful members of society, to the view that the "mentally deficient" should be sterilized? And then to the view that they should also be locked up?

AT THE TIME John Langdon Down was doing his groundbreaking work with the "feeble-minded," big changes were under way. The burden of care was slowly shifting from the family and church to the state. As the financial burden grew and the numbers housed in state institutions multiplied, resentment built up. The "feeble-minded," the argument ran, were out of control, reproducing at will, the cause of much crime and poverty. Something needed to be done.

The most virulent form of this line of thinking developed in the U.S. where studies purporting to prove that the "feeble-minded" were "breeding like maggots" became bestsellers. Richard Louis Dugdale's *The Jukes: A Study in Crime, Pauperism, Disease and Heredity* was heralded as proof that in a few short generations one sprawling family could produce an astonishing number of criminals, brothel-keepers, prostitutes, and "feeble-minded." And Henry Goddard's *The Kallikak Family: A Study in the Heredity of Feeble-Mindedness* published in 1912, supposedly showed that one young man's fling with a tavern girl had led, over a short time, to "an appalling amount of defectiveness."

So what was to be done? The answer was obvious. Prevent the "feeble-minded" from reproducing. What's important to understand now is that this wasn't the view of a small fringe group. Goddard was a leading psychologist in the U.S. And, speaking in the British House of Commons in 1910 of the thousands of "feeble-minded persons at large in our midst,"

Winston Churchill intoned, "There is no aspect more important than the prevention of the multiplication and perpetuation of this great evil." As fear of the "feeble-minded" continued to grow, support grew for the idea of sterilization without consent. In 1927 the U.S. Supreme Court made a landmark decision in the case of *Buck v. Bell*.

Carrie Buck, the court said, was a "feeble-minded" and "incorrigible" young woman—she'd had an illegitimate baby when she was eighteen and was the daughter of an equally immoral woman who'd been committed to the Virginia State Colony for Epileptics and Feebleminded. (Adopted as a young girl, Carrie was raped by the nephew of her adoptive family, a fact the court was not made aware of.) Soon after the birth of her daughter, Carrie, like her mother, was committed to the Virginia State Colony. Her daughter, Vivian, was adopted by the same family who'd adopted Carrie.

Carrie Buck arrived at the Virginia State Colony at a turning point. The state of Virginia had passed a new Racial Integrity Act that had been carefully crafted to follow a model law developed by a leader of the American eugenics movement, Harry Laughlin. Earlier laws allowing the sterilization of the "feeble-minded" had been either underused or overturned because they failed to give any rights to the person to be sterilized.

So Laughlin developed his Eugenical Sterilization Law as a model of due process. It targeted the "socially inadequate." Who were they? Anyone who "fails chronically in comparison with normal persons, to maintain himself or herself as a useful member of the organized social life of the state." But to make it abundantly clear who was being targeted, Laughlin set out a long list of "socially inadequate classes":

the feeble-minded

the insane

the "criminalistics"

the inebriate

the diseased

the blind

the deaf

the deformed, and

the dependent (including "orphans, ne'er-do-wells, the homeless, tramps and paupers")

Lawyers argued on behalf of Carrie Buck that Virginia's sterilization law denied her due process and equal protection of the law. If sterilized, she'd no longer have the same right as anyone else to have a child. Lawyers for the state presented evidence that not only were Carrie and her mother "feeble-minded," but her daughter, Vivian, examined by a social worker when the child was only seven months old, was also defective. The social worker testified that the baby did not look quite normal, though she couldn't say why she thought that. The U.S. Supreme Court had no trouble finding that Carrie Buck was "socially inadequate," someone who no doubt would produce more "socially inadequate offspring." Under Virginia's new law, Carrie Buck could legally be sterilized without her consent.

Justice Oliver Wendell Holmes Jr. delivered the court judgment that confirmed that state-authorized sterilization was legal:

We have seen more than once that the public welfare may call upon the best citizens for their lives. It would be strange if it could not call upon those who already sap the strength of the State... in order to prevent our being swamped with incompetence. It is better for all the world if, instead of waiting to execute degenerate offspring for crime or to let them starve for their imbecility, society can prevent those who are manifestly unfit from continuing their kind. The principle that sustains compulsory vaccination is broad enough to cover cutting the Fallopian tubes ... Three generations of imbeciles are enough.

Two Canadian provinces and thirty American states, as well as many European countries, passed laws that allowed the sterilization of people like Carrie Buck, both men and women. Many of those laws were later amended to allow sterilization to take place without consent.

In the U.S., it's estimated that seventy thousand people were sterilized under these laws. In Alberta, the first province to authorize sterilization of the "feeble-minded," over twenty-eight hundred people were sterilized. The actual number sterilized in the other province, British Columbia, is unknown. The records were either lost or destroyed.

IN 1933, THE newly elected German government noted what was happening in the U.S. and adopted many of the ideas and laws developed and tested by American eugenicists. (In 1936, eugenicist Harry Laughlin received an honorary doctorate from the University of Heidelberg.) Under the direction of Hitler's personal physician, the Reich Committee for the Scientific Registration of Severe Hereditary and Congenital Ailments approved the death of children with mental and physical disabilities.

As David Wright notes, children were told they were being sent to hospitals for special treatment, where they were "treated" by starvation, drug overdose, or lethal injection, while parents received the news that their child had died of pneumonia. Roughly five thousand children were killed this way.

In October 1939 this program was expanded to include adults with disabilities, resulting in between seventy thousand and ninety-five thousand disabled adults being killed. Facing mounting pressure from the Catholic Church and others who suspected what was going on, Hitler officially ended the program in 1941. Unofficially, it continued to the conclusion of the war. Many of the doctors involved in the program were transferred to the east to help with the "Final Solution to the Jewish Question."

Even the revelation of the full horror of Hitler's program of racial cleansing at the end of the war didn't stop many jurisdictions—Alberta, British Columbia, and California among them—from continuing their programs of sterilizing the mentally disabled without consent until well past the middle of the twentieth century.

It would then take several decades before the law would catch up to the public's revulsion.

IN CANADA IN 1986, "Mrs. E" applied to the court for permission to have her "mentally retarded" adult daughter, "Eve," sterilized. Mrs. E argued that neither she, a widow approaching sixty, nor Eve would be able to look after a baby. The case made its way to the Supreme Court of Canada, which refused to allow Eve to be sterilized without her consent. There was no evidence, it said, that Eve's mental or physical health would be harmed by not sterilizing her. And there were other reasons to be cautious:

The decision involves values in an area where our social history clouds our vision and encourages many to perceive the mentally handicapped as somewhat less than human. This attitude has been aided and abetted by now discredited eugenic theories whose influence was felt in this country as well as the United States.

The court concluded in *E. (Mrs.) v. Eve* that sterilization should never be authorized by a court for non-therapeutic reasons, unless the person to be sterilized consented.

THIS HISTORY, THE story of earlier Graces, is one that is little-known today. One I didn't know.

In a recent advertising campaign of the Canadian Down Syndrome Society, large billboards featured a young child with Down syndrome and two simple words: I Am. It wasn't until I had learned how the intellectually challenged were treated in the past that I appreciated the poignancy of these words.

• • •

SEVERAL MONTHS AFTER Kathleen's audition in New York, I pulled a fistful of mail from the box beside our front door. There among the junk mail and flyers was an official-looking letter from the theatre program Kathleen had applied to. I stepped back inside. "Katho! A letter for you." Kathleen had only arrived home from school a few minutes earlier and was in her room.

"Hang on, Mum!"

I held the letter up. Nothing gave away its verdict, though it was, I thought, more thick than thin. And thick was hopeful, wasn't it?

Kathleen skidded down the hall in her sock feet toward me. "Oh Mom, what is—" I held the letter out to her. Seeing the return address, she grabbed it from my hand and raced back to her room. I stared after her, not wanting to think how she'd handle rejection. Or how I would handle it. Would I be able to help her, or would I be a mess, my own disappointment flowing into hers?

In a few moments, Kathleen's door flew open, and she shrieked down the hall to me. "I made it! They said yes!"

I almost cried. She's done it, I thought. She's done it!

I grabbed Kathleen's hands and we hopped up and down, laughing and falling into each other.

ANOTHER FRIDAY AFTERNOON.

As Grace and I sit down at the table, Grace in front of her computer, Jessica sets a thermos of tea and a flowered mug down beside me. Today I sense something different. I glance up at her, but her face reveals nothing. Jessica picks up some papers from the opposite end of the table and holds them out to me. "This is the speech I told you about. The Japanese woman, Aya—"

Grace exhales noisily. "What that?" Her voice is harsh. Because of her hearing disability, Grace has trouble adjusting her volume when she speaks. And her mood, for reasons I can't fathom, seems to have abruptly darkened.

"Grace! It is not polite to interrupt."

"Oh yeah? You still wear apron."

"Grace." Jessica's voice holds a warning.

"Yeah, yeah." Staring at the screen, Grace clicks her mouse with a vengeance.

"Aya, she also is Down syndrome." Jessica smooths the

front of her apron. "She gave this speech at the World Down Syndrome Congress in Singapore a couple of years ago."

I glance at the title. "My Dream Came True," followed by "Everyone Is the Same Human, Same Life."

Grace abruptly interrupts. "I'm nervous!"

I look up from the speech. "You mean your piano recital?" For several weeks, Grace has told me about her struggle to master the two pieces she's going to play at her recital.

She nods. "They might throw flowers in my face!"

Jessica interjects. "Not enough practice."

"Apron!"

I resist the urge to smile at Grace's abbreviated insult. Hoping to head off a clash, I ask, "Why do you think they might throw flowers?"

Grace giggles. "Maybe they like my song?"

"I used to take piano lessons too," I confess, though I don't reveal how much I dreaded recitals, and how I often faked illness to avoid them. "I would have liked it if they'd thrown flowers at me."

"Yeah!" Grace grins now. "They throw flowers and I bow above them. Yeah!"

For a second, I slip into Grace's picture—Grace bowing after a perfect performance, the audience clapping and throwing flowers up on the stage at her feet. I see myself fling a flower up to Grace's beaming face.

The moment is broken as Jessica says, "Aya is coming to Vancouver. Maybe she and Grace can meet and talk." I glance up at Jessica. A look on her face holds me, though I'm not sure what it is—a new expectation, hopefulness?

"What!" Grace exhales loudly again.

I hold out the papers to Grace and she slowly reads the title. "'My Dream Came True.' What dream?"

"Want me to read it?"

Grace nods, and stares at the screen again, scrolling through her document as Jessica returns to the kitchen.

Although often sick as a child, Aya Iwamoto completed high school and went on to university. While there, she saw a TV program about Down syndrome and asked her father about it. "I had suspected I had something like that, but it was a great shock when I was told." Aya graduated from university, and her parents urged her to write a book about her accomplishments. But she didn't want to acknowledge her condition. "I cried bitterly," she wrote.

A loud snap interrupts me. I glance at Grace. She's slipped a hand under her shirt and is snapping her bra strap.

"Do you want me to stop?" I ask.

Abruptly Grace stands up, pushing her chair back roughly. She leans over her neat piles of papers, her precise lines of pens and pencils. In a second everything skews sideways, papers fluttering across the table, pens rolling off the edge of the table.

"Grace, what is it?"

Grace, her face dark, refuses to look at me. "My truth is too scary," she blurts. "I like to hide my real truth."

I'm stunned.

PART FOUR

Once upon a Time

IN HIS PROFOUNDLY moving yet angry book *The Body Si-lent,* Columbia University anthropologist Robert Murphy chronicles his transformation from a healthy middle-aged man to one forced by an inoperable spinal tumor to perma-nently use a wheelchair. He called it a "kind of extended anthropological field trip" into the world of the disabled.

Every culture, Murphy says, sorts reality into categories, and many cultures consider deviations from these categories to be dangerous. This is what makes the disabled so different from other kinds of "deviance," he says. They defy classifi-cation. As a result, Murphy writes, we "treat disability as a form of *liminality,*" a "kind of social limbo in which [the disabled] is left standing outside the formal social system." Liminality is similar "to darkness ... to an eclipse of the sun or the moon." And it's this state of being undefined, am-biguous, of being unable to be sorted into a neat and re-assuring category, Murphy says, that causes the disabled to be met with such unease.

With his unique perspective as both an able-bodied and a disabled man, Murphy describes how he once saw physical disability as something that happened to others, something that had no relevance to him. "A disabled person could en-ter my field of vision, but my mind would fail to register him—a kind of selective blindness quite common among people of our culture."

AS I READ these words, I recognize myself. Before I met Grace, I felt I'd never really seen anyone with Down syn-drome, even though I must have many times. Like Murphy,

I was blind to the Graces of my world.

As his own disability grew, Murphy became acutely sensitive to the social position of the disabled. He saw that social interactions with the disabled are often awkward, tense. Whatever the disability, it sits front and centre, making it difficult for even the most well meaning to have a normal encounter. The non-disabled person worries that he or she will say something that will hurt or offend the disabled person. The disabled person can either recognize the discomfort and try to relieve it, or ignore it. In both cases, the disability looms like a toxic fog between them, preventing a meaningful connection.

For Murphy, this issue wasn't just an academic inquiry. His own experience returning to the Columbia University campus where he'd taught for years, but this time in a wheelchair, affirmed his research. A colleague, noticing the reaction to him, called wheelchairs "portable seclusion huts."

But, Murphy argues, there's a big problem with all of this. While it may help to explain our aversion to the disabled, it doesn't deal with an undeniable fact. "You're just as alive as you always were," says Murphy, "and what are you going to do about it?"

The fact that you can't hide a visible disability forces every disabled person to make a fundamental choice: engage in life or withdraw from it. And a catalogue of the barriers to engagement makes the appeal of withdrawal clear. Laws intended to prevent discrimination can be circumvented. Employment is elusive. Affordable and accessible housing rare.

And Murphy cites another reason for withdrawal, one he only recognized when he was "one of them," as he put it. "Of all the psychological syndromes associated with disability," Murphy writes, "the most pervasive, and the most destructive, is a radical loss of self-esteem." He describes how he was ignored during stand-up gatherings at his university, most interactions taking place well above his head. His discomfort was so great he decided he'd only attend sit-down events.

Low self-esteem and feelings of inadequacy, Murphy writes, lead by a perverse route to guilt and shame. Instead of the usual path—wrongful act, followed by guilt, shame, and punishment—the disabled often follow a reverse route. Their disability is the punishment, which leads to guilt and shame, and the questions: What did I do to deserve this? What was my crime?

This constant attack on self-worth causes, Murphy says, another major factor in the life of the disabled: anger. That anger can be all-pervasive, a consuming bitterness at one's situation, or it can flare up sporadically in response to frustration or poor treatment. However it arises, Murphy says, that anger is aggravated by how the world interacts with the disabled. "They daily suffer snubs, avoidance, patronization, and occasional outright cruelty, and even when none of these occur, they sometimes imagine the affronts." And we allow the disabled very limited means to deal with their anger. If physically disabled, they can't stalk off as anyone else might. If mentally challenged, the ripping retort may never come to mind. "To make matters worse," Murphy writes, "they must comfort others about their condition. They cannot show fear, sorrow, depression, sexuality, or anger, for this disturbs the able-bodied."

And there's another factor that radically influences the lives of every disabled person. What Murphy calls an "embattled identity"—an identity where the disability dominates other characteristics, talents, and achievements. And that sense of stigma, of tainted identity, leads to an acute awareness of words and names. *Lady,* Murphy points out, is now thought of as patronizing, just as *coloured* fell out of favour long ago. Many people in wheelchairs, he says, are offended by the bluntness of *paralysis.* What Murphy finds most interesting about this debate is the debate itself: "It reveals a stance of defensiveness against belittlement that is seldom relaxed; it bespeaks a constant awareness of one's deficiencies."

I THINK OF all the times Grace and I met for coffee to work on her book. How sometimes she was greeted with looks that signalled unease or discomfort, sometimes an unfriendly or even outright hostile stare. How some cashiers were unable to look at Grace, and a few couldn't seem to hear her when she gave her order. How rare it was for someone to smile at her and say, "Hi, how are you?"

Grace always appeared to take this in stride, to not be bothered by it. To not even notice. But now I realize that's not how it is at all. She has noticed and taken in every unfriendly or hostile glance, every reaction that tells her she's invisible or unwanted. And she's concluded, logically I think, that her truth is too scary.

I feel a deep sadness mixed with guilt. Sad that Grace has been treated this way. That she feels that her truth needs to be hidden. And guilt because I've been someone who looked away, who couldn't see the person in front of me. How many people like Grace have I made feel the way Grace feels?

TODAY, AS GRACE stands beside the table, her pens and papers in disarray, Jessica appears from the kitchen. "She doesn't want to acknowledge the handicap."

Grace's laugh is harsh. "Yeah? You still wear apron." She slumps down into her chair and thumps her elbows on the table, her small hands pushed up against her face.

Grace stares fixedly at her screen. "Read," she commands.

So I continue to read about how Aya and her parents wrote a book together, about how Aya received letters from all over Japan when it was published. "People said my example gave them courage, that they cried reading my book, that they found hope for the future." Aya goes on to describe her work translating children's stories from English into Japanese, and how she hopes one day to be a librarian. She ends with a simple but profound statement: "I want to say once more to my parents, 'Thank you for giving birth to me.'"

Grace hunches in front of her computer, silent. Finally, she looks up at me. "She stole my idea! I want to be a librarian!"

●●●

AND THIS, I think, is what I see when Grace tells me she hates the word *Down*. It may be the name of a doctor who saw the potential in his patients with this condition. But over time, it's evolved into a word that limits, excludes, belittles. Code for dumb, stupid, retarded. A word that can prevent a life from beginning at all.

At the Canadian Down Syndrome Conference in 2011 in Vancouver, B.C., I attended a fascinating panel discussion. The moderator was Gail Williamson, a consultant with the California State Media Access Office and the "go-to person," as she describes herself, when film or TV projects call for an actor with Down syndrome or other disability. The two other panel members were Blair Williamson, Gail

Williamson's son, who's had roles on *CSI*, *ER*, and *Nip/ Tuck,* and Lauren Potter, who plays Becky Jackson on the TV megahit *Glee*. Both Williamson and Potter have Down syndrome.

Given the high-profile shows that both young actors had been on, I anticipated a positive discussion of their experiences. And that's what I heard, at least for the first fifteen minutes. But the mood changed as Lauren Potter described her work with the Special Olympics campaign to end the "R" word, a campaign that began in 2004 when the Special Olympics board of directors, in response to a request from some of its own athletes, adopted a resolution to eliminate the words "mentally retarded" from its website and materials. The movement gained momentum when the movie *Tropic Thunder* contained a scene that used the word *retard* as a joking way to poke fun. In response, Special Olympics launched its campaign "End the R Word," and President Obama signed a law in 2010 requiring the removal of the phrases "mentally retarded" and "mental retardation" from all federal statutes, replacing them with "intellectual disability."

An articulate and confident young woman, Lauren Potter broke down as she described what it felt like to hear the word *retarded* directed at her. Blair Williamson said he'd been called retarded too and also began to cry.

Almost a year later, I read an interview with Lauren Potter in *Entertainment Weekly* where she revealed the source of some of her hurt. At her public school, Potter said, the typical kids picked on her, making fun of her because she had Down syndrome, sometimes even pushing her down to the ground and forcing her to eat sand. Potter, the article notes, teared up as she recounted those early experiences.

Now, as I see Potter and Williamson break down on stage, I realize that the success of these two young people, as remarkable as it is, will never erase the hurt they have suffered.

• • •

SEVERAL MONTHS AFTER she'd received her letter of acceptance to theatre school, Kathleen and I returned to New York. This time we had a different mission: to find all the items on the list issued by her university—by my count, forty-seven seemed essential—and somehow cart them back to her tiny, built-for-one-but-occupied-by-two dorm room. It was mid-morning, late August heat rising from the sidewalks as we joined a crush of shoppers flocking into The Store. Bed Bath and Beyond. The store where you can buy everything you need, Kathleen's new friends at her residence have told her. And they deliver!

I held the list of items Kathleen must have to survive her first year. Sheets, twin and long, pillow cases, and bed risers so her dorm bed could be lifted up and she could shove plastic storage bins under it. I felt tired already, looking at the mountains of stuff, mostly plastic or cheap synthetics, that had crossed the ocean and the continent so we, the harried parents of nervous first-year students could paw over them, ponder thread count and colour while trying not to think about who might be sleeping in those sheets. And find the essential bathroom accessories. What eighteen-year-old needed bathroom accessories? Our supersized cart was still empty, and I was already thinking, *Bed Bath and Ridiculously Beyond.*

"Come on," my daughter urged as she led me through the maze of aisles, "let's go buy some towels." Kathleen is obsessed with washing her face. A careless comment by my husband at the depth of her teenaged acne tipped her into a "one fresh towel every day" habit. I followed her, man-oeuvring the cart like an awkward boat. We passed through bedding, where I snatched a package of sheets from a stack without slowing. A sign told me these were twin and long and that's all I needed to know. Kathleen disappeared around a hanging display of quilts. I sped up. If we lost each other, it'd be a long distance call with our Canadian cellphones.

I wheeled around a corner. Over a nearby low table of white towels, huge red sale banners announced Best Buy! A thick knot of shoppers crowded around. This must be where the real bargains were.

I manoeuvred my buggy closer, edging into the outer circle of shoppers, Kathleen beside me. As I looked between heads and shoulders, I realized it wasn't the towels that were the attraction.

A few feet in front of the circle of shoppers, a grey-haired woman was taking short, awkward steps backward around the table of towels. "No, no, no," she muttered, her voice low, urgent. A squat, strong-looking woman in her late thirties pursued her. The younger woman took stiff, determined steps, making deep, angry sounds that seemed to tangle in her throat. I studied the older woman's face. It was pulled tight, as if she was trying desperately not to let her fear show. More steps, awkward, small, hurried. The older woman held up her hand, palm out, a signal, it seemed to me, that she hoped the younger woman would recognize. Something about the hand, the way it was raised, the way it was ig-nored, made me think they were mother and daughter, caught in a moment of public agony. I searched the daugh-ter's face. Small eyes, flattish forehead, thick tongue. With a sick feeling, I realized she had Down syndrome.

Abruptly, the daughter lunged forward, thick fingers swiping close to her mother's face. The mother jerked back, teetering off balance for a long moment. As a stack of towels toppled over, the crowd sucked in a collective gasp. A clammy fear gripped me. Someone needed to do something. But what? Could I do anything? I stared at the daughter. She was much heavier than I was and looked like she could swat me away with one hand. My stomach tightened. Behind me, a man muttered, "Jesus. That retard's gonna get her."

His words slammed into me. He's right, I thought. She's crazy. Dangerous. A retard. Someone needs to stop her.

I turned to Kathleen. "Let's get out of here."

We abandoned our cart. As we walked away, I saw two baby-faced security guards hurrying along the aisle. They looked like college students, no older than Kathleen, stuffed into dark dress pants and white shirts, the shiny plastic name tags pinned to their chests their only claim to authority.

Outside, the heat walloped us. We walked silently, our heads down. After a few blocks, a stairwell appeared. The subway line that would take us back to Kathleen's dorm. We descended into the gloom to the faint squeal of a departing train. Aside from a couple of teenage boys at the far end, the platform was deserted. We sat down on a scarred metal bench.

AS WE HEARD the low throb of an approaching train, Kathleen leaned her head against my shoulder. Her long brown hair fell onto my arm, partially covering her face. I brushed it back, a gesture she probably would have resisted a year ago, but here, now, she accepted. Abruptly, the defining and unforgettable line from Marsha Norman's 'night, Mother monologue that Kathleen rehearsed so intensely on our last visit popped into my head. *I am what became of your child.* Although I doubted that the mother we'd just encountered had ever heard that line, in the situation we'd just witnessed, the line felt like a sentence, a confinement to a lifetime of trying to manage her unpredictable, sometimes dangerous, daughter. But had it once been different for that mother and daughter? Had they walked the streets of their city, talking and laughing, just being together? Had her daughter slowly and insidiously developed something in addition to her disability—a mental illness, perhaps—that pulled disturbance and fear into their lives? Was that mother now struggling to hold competing images of her daughter in her mind—the daughter who responded to the upheld hand, and the distraught, menacing daughter we'd just seen?

Later, back in my hotel room, I thought of Grace. Of her pens and pencils in their neat rows, her notebooks, her ability to imagine herself into a story. Of how different she was from the out-of-control daughter Kathleen and I had seen earlier.

Why had those words—*She's crazy, dangerous, a retard, someone needs to stop her*—popped so easily into my head? Even now, after knowing Grace, after realizing how ignorant I was before meeting Grace? Why were revulsion and fear my default position? I was sure that daughter was dangerous, to her mother at least. Whether she'd try to hurt anyone else was impossible to know, though it looked in that moment as though she'd lash out at anyone who tried to stop her. I realized that what Kathleen and I had seen was, in Robert Murphy's terms, a moment when it felt like the dark shadow of an eclipse fell over all of us, strangers united only by the coincidence of witnessing something terrifying unfold in one small section of a huge store. Another aisle over and we'd have had no idea what was happening. Life there would have been predictable, ordinary, much easier to decipher.

From where we'd stood, mesmerized, it was hard to know for sure what we'd seen. Was it really a mother and daughter? Was the daughter mentally ill as well as intellectually disabled? Or in a rage? It was impossible to know. Uncertainty and fear cast a dark shadow, making it hard to see clearly.

But my fear had been real. A gut-twisting fear that that young woman could easily turn on any of us. Or on me.

●●●

AND THE FEAR I felt that day in New York evoked a twinge, a faint memory of earlier fear. I thought back, trying to find the details that would help me remember. Where had I been? Who had I been with? I turned over the few details that came to mind—a long subway ride at night, an upset young man. And then it flooded back to me.

When our oldest son, David, was in his final year of high school, we went to an information night held at the new Surrey campus of one of the local universities. The event was to promote a new program in digital design, something David thought he might be interested in. Instead of driving for almost an hour to get there, we took the gleaming new rapid transit train—the SkyTrain, it was called, since most of it was well above ground level—that threaded out through Vancouver and over the Fraser River to Surrey.

At the event, we poked around the exhibits, but I sensed that David was uncomfortable, that something was making him uneasy. Maybe it was the bright and almost overly enthusiastic student hosts, or maybe it was the professors, who seemed to be standing back and sizing up prospective students. After a quick pass through the exhibits, David and

I returned to the nearby station and hopped on the train. The car was almost empty, the two of us near the front, a few others farther back.

As the train pulled smoothly out of the station, I thought of asking David why he seemed uncomfortable, but I knew if I waited I'd hear more than if I peppered him with questions. So we rode in silence, each of us staring out the now dark windows. Squat buildings rolled past, falling away as the train lifted up on the approach to the bridge. Soon we were on the wide span that crossed the river, the water a black pit below us.

Maybe it was our silence, the lack of many people in the car, but we soon became aware of what seemed like soft sounds of distress from behind us, punctuated by louder sounds—bursts of laughter, slurred words. I glanced at David, to see if he'd noticed it. He raised an eyebrow and together we turned to look back. A few seats behind us, a teenaged male, maybe sixteen or seventeen, was clearly upset. I stared at him for a moment. Something was not quite right about him. His eyes too close together. I realized he was mentally challenged.

Farther back, a group of four young men, all looking like they were in their early twenties, sprawled across several seats, legs wide apart, ball caps tilted far back on their heads. They'd found something hilarious to laugh about, their loud guffaws rolling up the car toward us. Their words were slurred, but I thought I could make out a few. *Stupid. Idiot. Retard.* I glanced at David. He'd heard too. He looked down for a moment, then said, his voice low, "Something's gonna happen, I can tell."

I glanced back again. The teenager's face was red and blotchy, and he was half-turned in his seat, staring back at the young men. David was right. Any moment that teenager was going to get up and who knew what would happen then.

What could we do? The young men at the back of the car were drunk or high. Out of control. And there were four of them.

We rode on. I searched along the walls of the car. There it was, the emergency call button. Would anything happen if I hit it? Would the train jerk to a stop between stations, leaving us stranded? I scrunched down in my seat, not knowing what to do. Fear crept down my spine, making me feel almost queasy.

The train slowed to a stop at the next station. Abruptly, David stood up. "Come on," he said, "let's change cars."

I stood up and as I did, I caught the eye of the teenager behind us. I motioned with my hand, come with us, and he stood up. The three of us left the car and entered the one behind.

The teenager sat down across from us, his hands shaking. "Th ... those guys," he said. "Calling names. I hate that." His face still red, he perched on the edge of his seat, his fingers knotting and unknotting.

The train pulled away. "How far are you going?" I asked. He named a station long before ours. "We're going past there," I said. "We'll stay with you until you get off."

He nodded, short bobs of his head, like someone who wants to believe, but is not at all sure. "Okay," he said, "okay." But I could feel his fear and how it was something he lived with.

The train slid through the outskirts of Vancouver, where the noisy young men spilled out onto the platform. The teenager, who'd told us his name was Brad, stared after them. "Assholes," he muttered. A few stops later, he stood up. "Thanks," he said. He walked out of the car and in seconds he'd vanished into the crowd on the platform.

It would take some time before I'd realize that I'd glimpsed opposing sides of the same disturbing picture. In the New York store, I'd been part of the small huddle of shoppers who'd witnessed the young woman who seemed determined to attack her mother, afraid that she might turn on one of us. On the SkyTrain, I'd seen the fear of the threatened teenager and had identified with him. Each time, fear was like a toxin, making me smaller, less able to deal with the situation.

ONE NIGHT IN early June, Grace's younger brother, Albert, calls me.

"Judy," he begins, "I've been formatting Grace's book and I have a question."

I've only seen Albert a few times in all my visits to Grace's house. A computer science student, he's usually been at classes or studying. And the very few times I've seen him with Grace, he's seemed impatient, bursting to be somewhere else. Much like any other brother.

A few weeks earlier, I'd told my friend Madelyne that Grace was almost finished her book. She'd looked at me and said, "Wouldn't it be great to have a book launch for her?"

I thought back to when Madelyne had first asked me to meet Grace. How impossible it seemed then that someone like Grace could write anything, let alone a book. How every week that we'd met, Grace had produced new writing, and every week we'd worked together to revise and polish her writing. How we'd talked about many writing issues— point of view, tense choices, how to keep a story moving— that I'd once thought would be impossible to talk about with Grace.

But now, I realize that Madelyne must have suggested

a launch to Jessica, because here was Albert, formatting Grace's book.

"That's great, so—"

"Yeah, my parents want to publish it. So I was thinking—" Albert paused. "This is a real book Grace has written, so it should look like one, don't you think?"

Yes! I want to shout, it is a book, a real one! But my experience with my own children tells me to play it down, not up.

"Yeah, that'd be good. How did you like Grace's book?"

"I didn't read it. But my girlfriend read it all and she really liked it."

"So what are you wondering about?"

"Well, we've got these illustrations now and if I try to reduce them to the size of a normal paperback, they don't work. So if I keep it at 8½ by 11, is that okay with you?"

A couple of weeks ago, Jessica had told me that Mary Baker, a member of Grace's church and a children's book illustrator, had been working on some illustrations for Grace's book.

"Whatever size you think will work is fine with me," I say. "What are the illustrations like?"

"Pretty cool, I guess. Hey, gotta go. I'll get Mom to show you, okay?"

• • •

ANOTHER FRIDAY. AS I walk down Grace's driveway, her front door opens. There's Grace, framed in the doorway. I smile and wave and she gives a hop as she waves back. When I'm at her door, she hops again, several times. "I have something to show you! Come quick!"

I slip on my pink slippers as Grace motions me to hurry

into the living room. There, spread out in a neat line on the floor, are seven large watercolours. The illustrations for her book.

Grace drops to her knees in front of the first painting, patting the floor beside her. Kneeling, Grace and I shuffle along the line of paintings, bending over them one by one. With a light, almost whimsical touch, Mary has created an Asiatic Cinderella-Grace with long, dark hair, a fierce bun-headed stepmother with dangerously long nails, one chubby stepsister, and a second thin, slightly dissipated-looking one. Prince Ronald is handsome in a prince-like way, with a serious, attentive face.

We stop in front of the last painting. Standing beside Prince Ronald, Cinderella-Grace holds one of her three babies. The other two babies play together on a blanket on the ground at their parents' feet. In the background is the golden castle and the royal helicopter, ready to take Cinderella-Grace and her husband on their next mission as international spies. I think of the ending Grace found for her book: *After several years as international spies, Prince Ronald and I become known far and wide. Prince Ronald becomes the royal grand golden crown King, and I become the royal grand golden crown Queen, and we live in our royal grand golden crown castle with our three beautiful daughters, who are doing well in their training to become spies.*

"Grace, these are fantastic!"

"I know. I really love them." Grace stands up and I follow to our usual spot at the dining room table.

Jessica appears from the kitchen, her hands cupped around a thermos of oolong tea. "I called some printers to get estimates to print Grace's book. I think I've found one." She smiles. "I ask Albert to format the book for the printer, and—"

"He called and told me," I say. "And these"—I wave my hand at the line of paintings—"these are so wonderful."

Jessica smiles again. "Mary found a way to make Grace's book alive." She sets the thermos down beside me. "And Madelyne from our church said they will have a book launch."

"Did she suggest a date?"

"She said July is best."

Grace looks up at her mother. "Why? Why is July best?"

"It's when the church lounge is available."

"Why not next week? Why do we have to wait?"

"Your book is not ready, Grace."

"Oh. Well, tell Albert, hurry up!"

Jessica smiles. "Okay, okay, I will tell Albert."

Grace thumps her elbows on the table. "Jeez!"

●●●

ABOUT THE SAME time, I learn that the World Down Syndrome Congress will be held in Vancouver in August. And that there may be an opportunity for Grace to display her book there.

I let Jessica know, and she wastes no time getting in touch with the congress organizers:

Hello, My name is Jessica Chen.

As I am planning to give a free copy of my daughter Grace's newly finished book *Cinderella-Grace, Vancouver Princess,* to the representative of each country, so, may I have the name list of registration, also the name of representative of each country? Then I can help to put this book into their registration package on Tuesday Aug. 22.

It is a pride of both Grace and Canada.

Hope I can hear from you ASAP.

Jessica

With a flurry of e-mails, it's arranged. Grace will give a copy of her book to a representative of each country and will be able to display her book, too. David and Albert are pressed into helping get the display ready.

• • •

A COUPLE OF weeks before the book launch, in early July, Jessica calls me.

"Judy, we are ready to print the book, and we wonder how many we need." She pauses. "Do you think twenty-five will be enough?"

The launch of Grace's book will be near the end of July, a time when I know many people will be away. "I think that'll be enough," I say. "Can I help you with anything to get ready?"

"No, we will have everything ready, thanks."

"And how's Grace?"

Jessica laughs. "Grace is very excited. Maybe a bit nervous. But I tell her, you will be there. David and I will be there. Albert, too, I hope. And we invite Ronald, but I don't know if he will be there."

I recognize a familiar worry in her voice, one I can identify with, that her daughter will be hurt; that at this stage, there's only so much she can do to prevent it.

• • •

THE DAY OF the launch. I pull into the church parking lot, which I'm surprised to see is more than half full, given that it's a cloudless day, already hot by Vancouver standards.

I walk along the hallway to the lounge. This is where the launch will be held at the end of today's service. A large, airy room with soft armchairs and sofas, bookshelves along one side and a couple of larger serving tables at the far end, it's completely empty except for Jessica and David. Grace is nowhere to be seen. Jessica, wearing a tailored, cream-coloured suit, turns to me as I walk in. "Oh, Judy, I am so glad you are here."

David looks up from the cardboard box he's unpacking. Copies of Grace's book. He hands one to me. I take it, feel the smooth cover, and flip it open. Here is the preface I wrote, Grace's biography, a few testimonials about Grace, and a dedication by Grace:

To my loving family
For their unconditional
Devotion and love.
Attentive Father—David
Relentless Mother—Jessica
Charming Brother—Albert

David looks at me. "You like it?"

I nod, my eyes filling. What can I say? It's well done, beautiful, but more than that, it's real. Grace's book exists.

As I stand there, unable to speak for a moment, Albert walks in. Taller than his father, he wears a light-coloured dress shirt and dark pants. He nods to me. "Hi, Judy. Did you see Grace? She keeps disappearing."

Jessica looks up. "She keeps going back into the service, to see how many people are there, but I think she can't count them all."

"It doesn't matter," says Albert. "What's she worried

about? We have enough books." At that, Grace walks into the room. She's wearing her dark blue Titanic dress, her hair pulled back from her face. I wave and she skips over to me, wrapping her arms around me in a fierce hug. "Hey, Grace," I say, loosening her arms when it seems she's not about to, "you look great." She smiles, but it's a wan smile. "How are you feeling?"

"Okay."

"Just okay?"

We've moved around to the other side of the tables now where I slide the microphone stand along a few inches, trying to make it more centred. I give it a tap, but it doesn't respond.

Grace runs her tongue over her lower lip and looks up at me. "I'm nervous," she whispers.

I take her hand. "Me, too."

"Really?"

"Really." I am nervous, more than I thought I'd be.

From the hallway, the sound of the final hymn floats in. For the past couple of Sundays, the minister has announced that Grace's book launch will be today. Now, the room begins to hum as people wander in. I glance over to the double-wide doors. Madelyne's there, watching out for older members of the congregation, the ones she knows will need help finding a place to sit down.

Snatches of conversation blur together—*Have you started yet? She'll be signing them later. My granddaughter has it, too. Where do you want these?*—interrupted by the abrupt cry of a very small boy in his father's arms.

"Oh, for crying out loud!" Grace says, and at that moment, we learn the microphone has been turned on. A short burst of laughter from the crowd and Grace turns to me. "Why are they laughing?"

"They just weren't expecting to hear your voice yet."

People are crowding through the doors now. I stretch up as far as I can. The hallway outside is jammed with people wanting to get in. Madelyne guides two elderly women, one on each arm, to one of the sofas.

"I'm nervous," Grace says again, her face close to mine. I look down as she wipes her palms against her dress. This is the moment, I realize, when Grace needs to know, to feel in her body, that she can get through this. A moment I've often experienced with Kathleen. Many times before the start of one of her plays, we've stood facing each other in the same way, her eyes silently asking me to will her confidence to return. But what can I say today that will help Grace through this? The phrases that can soothe in these moments, ones I've often used before—you can do it, it'll be okay—seem inadequate, trite even. And I feel an unsettling nervousness, too. My initial worry that Grace's book launch would be overlooked has transformed into a bigger worry that the audience will be too large, overwhelming for both of us.

I place my hands on Grace's shoulders. For the briefest of moments, it's as if I feel my mother's hands holding my face and hear her say, "You can be anything, Judy."

I look at Grace. "When you wrote your book," I say, "it took a lot of courage. You can do this, Grace. I know you can."

Grace stares up at me, as if she doesn't really believe what I'm saying.

"Are you sure?" she asks.

I nod as confidently as I can. In a moment, the room falls silent.

"Good morning, everyone," Madelyne says, microphone in one hand. "This is an amazing day. A kind of miracle day." Madelyne pauses. "Grace has been helping here at the church for a long time. She's a wonderful helper, always on time. And for years she's carried her journal with her. One day, many months ago now, she confided in me that she wanted to be a writer."

Madelyne briefly describes how Grace and I met and worked together, how Mary Baker created the illustrations, how Grace's parents decided to publish her book.

"And now," Madelyne says, "it still seems unbelievable, but we're here to celebrate Grace and her book." She looks at Grace. "Grace, can you say a few words?"

Grace looks up, startled, as if this is an unexpected idea. But the last time I was at Grace's house, Jessica, Grace and I had talked about this moment as we sat in the dining room going over the plans for the launch.

"Are you okay talking first?" I'd asked Grace. "You're the person everyone will want to hear most."

Grace had nodded. "Okay, sure," she'd said, with the easy confidence of knowing this day was still a week away.

David gently nudges his daughter forward and whispers in her ear. Grace slides her tongue across her lips and lifts the microphone.

"Thank you..." She stops to clear her throat loudly. "Thank you for coming to my magical fairy tale." A sympathetic murmur from the crowd, cut through with a few nervous laughs. Will this fall apart before it's even begun? The small boy whose cry startled me earlier turns his head and leans against his father's shoulder, as if he's trying to make sense of this. I see that he also has Down syndrome.

Bending close to Grace's ear, I whisper, "Take a deep breath." She nods and grips the microphone with one hand, her book in the other. The room falls silent again.

"*Once upon a time,*" Grace begins, "*there was me.*" Her voice low, Grace reads slowly, pausing every few minutes to run her tongue over her lips. *My name is Cinderella-Grace Wei Ju Chen.*

I search the faces of the audience. Many are the older women who keep this church alive. Who among them, I wonder, is the mother, grandmother, or aunt of someone like Grace? And who is here out of curiosity, a desire to see something unusual?

I am twenty-four years old and I have straight black hair. I have a very soft and smooth silky face. During the winter, my mother has been ill for a very long time and her face is turning white as a sheet. She knows she is dying soon.

Grace reads her fictional mother's last words to her with deep emotion.

Why don't you go into the elegant red rose garden and find a white angel bird? When you see one, you will think of me, and how much I love you. I'll be watching over you with a red rose kiss on your forehead, my dear princess.

Grace lowers her book as she looks up at her audience. "I always try to write from my deepest heart," she says. "About beauty, truth and—" she glances around the hall, as if she might spot a prince among the grandmothers—"romance." A burst of laughter. "Oh, for crying out loud!" she exclaims again.

As Grace finishes her reading, the audience applauds long and enthusiastically. She looks bewildered for a second, then beams. "Oh yeah!"

Grace thrusts the microphone at me and as I take it, I feel it slip in my hand. Grace's nervous sweat is now in my palm. I look out at the audience. "This is a day Grace and I have dreamed about for over eleven months."

I stop, not sure if I have the courage to be honest with my part of the story. How do I say here, now, to these expectant faces, that I didn't want to meet Grace? That I didn't think we could talk about writing? That I thought Grace would be stupid, maybe dangerous? That I was afraid to meet her?

I hold up Grace's book. "I'd like to read the preface to Grace's book," I say. "It explains better than I can now, how we met and began working together."

As I read, a softened version of my part of the story comes out—how I stood at Grace's front door telling myself to leave; how the door opened without my knocking; how Grace held up her dark blue dress and told me, *This is what I'll wear.* How I realized that Grace wanted to tell her own story.

I feel honoured to have been able to work with Grace. As she has written her story of transformation, she has transformed my view of her and all others with Down syndrome. Without warning, I choke up. The room is silent. Grace leans her head against my shoulder. "It's okay," she says, her words amplified by the microphone. A low murmur of laughter gives me a few seconds to pull myself together and I read my last sentence: *Thank you, Grace, for helping me become a better human being.*

With relief, I pass the microphone along to Mary Baker.

"When I read the first sentence of Grace's book, 'Once upon a time, there was me—'" Mary looks up at the crowd—"I knew then this was a special story. And Grace told me her book was about love, beauty, and—"

Grace leans close to the microphone. "Romance!"

Another burst of laughter. "And romance," Mary confirms.

The microphone makes its way along to Jessica and a hush falls over the room. She wraps both hands around it. David glances at her. From outside, the heavy beat of a boom box momentarily fills the room.

"When Grace was born, I never thought there would be

a day like this." Jessica smiles. She thanks everyone who has helped Grace with her book.

When it's Albert's turn he says, "Grace has banned me from reading her book." Another nervous laugh ripples through the crowd. Is Albert about to spill some brotherly beans?

He holds up a copy of the book and says, "It's hard to believe, but this is Grace's book." He shakes his head, as if he still can't believe his sister's accomplishment. "She worked hard to do this. Congratulations, Grace."

Grace groans. "Oh, God!"

Last to speak is Grace's father, David. He speaks hesitant-ly but with a strong voice. "Grace like the TV, the movies—*Cinderella, Peter Pan*—"

"—And Mary-Kate and Ashley," Grace interjects.

David continues. "And she always dream to be a writer." He shifts the microphone to his other hand. "I always tell Grace, don't daydream. But today, her dream come true." He pauses, glancing down before he looks up again. "Today, I share my happiness with you. As a father. Thank you."

Madelyne announces that Grace will sign copies of her book. A small frenzy erupts as people jostle into a straggly line in front of the stack of books that sits at the end of one table.

Albert pulls a chair up so Grace can sit while she signs copies of her book. One of the elderly church members, a woman with a polished cane who's managed to manoeuvre to the front of the line, asks, "Do you want me to open the books so they're ready?"

Albert announces in a loud voice, "You have to be patient with Grace." There's a murmur of disappointment as the books run out before the end of the line. Jessica starts a list of names of those who want to order a copy.

One of the church women slides a large cake—"Congratulations, Grace!" it exclaims in bright yellow frosting—onto the far end of the table and begins to separate a stack of paper plates. David says, "We will print more books."

An elderly woman bends forward as Grace signs her name. "Well done, Grace," she says, her voice low.

Madelyne announces, "I forgot to mention—the books are fifteen dollars each. And Jessica and David want me to tell you that the proceeds will go to the Caring Ministry."

There's a brief murmur as the crowd takes in this news. An excited din fills the room, punctured by Grace calling out, her voice loud and urgent: "Quick! Cut the cake!"

Later, when everyone has left and it's just Grace and her family and me left in the lounge, Grace walks over to me, holding a paper plate weighted down with a large slice of yellow cake.

"What do you think?" I ask. "Are you happy with how your book launch went?" Grace stares out at the empty room and nods, almost absent-mindedly.

"What are you thinking, Grace?"

"My prince," she says. "Ronald, I invite him, but he didn't come today." She looks up at me and I see hurt in her eyes. Fiction, even when it succeeds as it has today, I realize, is no substitute for reality.

LATER, JESSICA WILL tell me that she invited Ronald and his family, but they decided not to come to the book launch. Now, I'm unaware of that. I put my arm around Grace. "You'll have to sign a copy for Ronald."

Grace brightens. "Yes, I want to do that."

She gives a small skip as Albert calls out. "Grace! Are you going to help clean up, or what?"

- - -

THE WORLD DOWN Syndrome Congress. It's being held in Vancouver for the first time in August 2006. Organized by Down Syndrome International, a U.K. charitable organization, and hosted every three years by a different national organization, the congress draws delegates with a range of interests—medical researchers, companies and individuals promoting services and products, and those with Down syndrome and their families.

As I'll see over the next few days, it's a way for people from all over the world to connect, to compare notes, to draw inspiration from each other, and, as Grace would say, "just hang out."

The first morning of the congress, David drops Jessica, Grace, and me off at the front entrance to Canada Place, the enormous conference facility on the Vancouver waterfront that is the site for the event. Grace skips ahead, too excited to walk. Around us are families and other delegates, but what's striking are the number of people with Down syndrome. Not a surprise, obviously, but it makes me realize that here Grace is the norm and Jessica and I are not. That switch, from being part of the norm to being the "other," experienced by anyone who travels far enough afield, can be unsettling. For a few moments, I feel as if I'm in a foreign land—I am the "other"—where those who live here are filling the high-ceilinged foyer with an excited buzz.

WE FIND OUR way to Exhibit Hall B, an enormous room where all the displays, including Grace's, will be set up. All of the exhibitors, Jessica has told me, will have their own display board. Posters and pamphlets can be displayed on it, but nothing must stick out from it, and there'll be no room to sell books near the display.

David meets us near Grace's assigned place. He has a large rolled-up poster about Grace's book and a measuring stick and tape. As he and Jessica begin planning how to position Grace's poster, Grace stands back, taking in the hum of activity around her. "What do you think?" I ask.

Grace shrugs. "I don't know." She gestures at her parents, who are carefully measuring their display space. "Jeez, just put it up. Let's go!" Grace speaks in a soft voice. I know she wants to get back to the main foyer where she spotted some friends earlier. And in a short while, she'll join the program for young adults while I attend some of the other sessions.

"Won't be long," I say.

"Brother," Grace mutters. Like anyone her age, she knows this is not where the excitement is.

Jessica and David stand back. The poster is up. It shows an enlarged copy of the cover of Grace's book and details of how to obtain a copy from Jessica.

Within minutes, a young woman who's been putting up her own display with her parents' help walks over. About Grace's age, she stops in front of Grace's display.

"You wrote a book?" she asks.

"Yeah!"

"Cool. I write poems." She gestures to her display. "Want to see?"

Grace nods and walks with the young woman to her display. Later, I'll learn this young woman has a rare form of Down syndrome called mosaic, where only some cells have an extra chromosome, resulting in an IQ typically 10 to 30 points higher than the average IQ of someone with Down syndrome.

Grace studies the poems then points to one of them. "This one here," she says, planting her finger on it, "I really like it."

The conference is a whirlwind of keynote speeches, breakfast talks, breakout sessions, medical/scientific discussions, and chance hallway meetings. There's a high pitch of excitement coupled with a fiercely optimistic bent. The current tagline of the Canadian Down Syndrome Society, Celebrate Being, is everywhere.

When I meet Michael Shaw, the chairperson of the Canadian Down Syndrome Society, I ask him about that cheery slogan. Does he think it will change anyone's views?

Shaw, a university professor and the father of two daughters, one with Down syndrome, leans forward, an intense look on his face. "We've got one planet. There's not a lot of other options out there for us. We need to see so much more clearly how much we're the same."

Shaw tells me his daughter Sydney is seven. When I tell him about working with Grace, about how she said that her "real truth is too scary," he sits back.

"I see what Sydney's future could be like, and it is a scary world. I figure I've got ten to fifteen years to change the world. Do I lie awake at night thinking I won't get it done? Yeah. It's terrifying." He smiles. "That's why I love coming to these conferences. They energize me for the whole year."

And there's the answer, at least for parents like Michael Shaw. Call the Celebrate Being slogan whatever you want. To parents, to anyone who's seen the gap between how the world sees Sydney and Grace and how they see themselves, this slogan is an exquisitely succinct summary of fact and hope: We are here. Let us live the fullest life possible. Celebrate Our Being.

SHAW SUGGESTS I meet some of the older "self-advocates." These are people with Down syndrome who've been selected from across Canada to sit on Voices at the Table Advocacy, or VATTA, recently formed by the Canadian Down Syndrome Society. This committee, Shaw explains, advises the CDSS on the issues the society really needs to pay attention to.

That afternoon, I meet Dale Froese and Laurel Griffin, both charter members of VATTA, in the CDSS hospitality suite on the twenty-fifth floor of the Pan Pacific Hotel.

Dale Froese, thirty, is a happy-looking young man who doesn't wait for me to ask a question. "My passion," he says, leaning forward, giving me an intense look, "is to educate people about Down syndrome, to talk about what it's been like."

"What was it like for you?" I ask.

"School was very inclusive. I finished and graduated with a Dogwood diploma. But it was lonely growing up. My sister had her friends, and my brother didn't get along with me when I was a kid. I wanted to have friends, but I didn't because we kept moving. And I was the only one in my class who had a disability, and the only one in my family. I was the special one, for some reason."

Dale plants his elbows on his knees and looks down. The moment of silence stretches out. But when he looks up, a big smile lights up his face.

"I've been married for eight years. We rent a condo from my father and do our own grocery shopping, cooking, laundry. We have a lot of friends. That really helps us a lot." He grins. "Now I'm married, I have to learn to understand the woman's perspective. Man." He shakes his head. "It's tough!" He laughs. "My wife has been a great influence to me. We started the Angels Support Group in Kelowna. At first, there were five of us and now it's grown to over thirty. We want to go to Calgary next, then to every province."

"What does your group do?"

"We meet every two months and talk about issues, problems. We help each other and go on outings." Dale looks at me with his open, friendly face. "And I work. I have two jobs. I'm being trained as a florist's assistant, learning how to prep flowers."

"And the other job?"

"I dance on the street, do hip hop. For Little Caesar's Pizza. Like this," he says, jumping up. He sways side to side, his hands motioning the beat as he raps, his voice strong and rhythmic:

My name is Dale
I like to wail
on the street!

AT FIFTY-TWO, LAUREL Griffin is the oldest person I've met with Down syndrome. Short and compact, her round face framed by grey hair, she speaks in a clear but sometimes hesitant voice.

"I was supposed to die before I turned fourteen," she says. "The doctor told my mum put her in an institution. But my mum, she said no. When I was six, I went to school." She pauses, looking out the window, where the dark green of Stanley Park juts into a blue sky. A floatplane taking off from the harbour buzzes, gnat-like.

"How was school?"

Laurel's mouth pulls sideways. "Let's put it this way, it was not very good. The teachers taught us by our handicaps, not by what we knew. It was a school for people like me, but it was very bleak. So I stayed home and the school I had was there. Two family friends, teachers who didn't have their tickets, taught me."

Laurel describes moving to Vancouver once she finished school, working in a shelter, and living in a suburban group home. Her life comes out in pieces, long gaps not accounted for. Now, she tells me, "My boyfriend lives next door. Our families know each other. But we're not going to get married. Where we live, we hear sirens all the time. We have to be careful who we talk to and keep our doors locked all the time."

Laurel stares out the window again. Soon it will be time to take the elevator down and find the meeting room where the VATTA panel discussion will take place. "Once," she says, "I was working in the library, and I heard two girls at the back talking. They were making statements putting down mentally retarded people. I walked back there and told them, 'Lots of people have handicaps, so don't use those labels. You get labels on jars, not on people.'"

LAUREL'S STATEMENT CONJURES the many labels I've encountered in researching and writing this. Words that all began with a specific meaning:

Cretin. From the French, meaning Christian. Based on the belief that the intellectually challenged, like small children, were incapable of sinning, and so were Christ-like, Christian.

Imbecile. Also French, meaning weak-minded.

Idiot. From the Greek word, *idiotes*, meaning one in a private station, a layman, or ignorant.

Did the Greeks somehow, through their choice of word, recognize the loneliness of the mentally challenged? As late as 1970, the definition of the word *idiot* included those with Down syndrome.

Retard. From the French word *retarder*, to slow or loiter.

Feeble-minded. Deficient in intelligence.

Moron. A word invented by Henry Goddard, a leading U.S. psychologist in the early twentieth century. Someone with an IQ between 51 and 70 (as opposed, in Goddard's hierarchy, to an idiot, whose IQ was between 0 and 25, and an imbecile, whose IQ fell between 26 and 50).

In spite of the origin of each word, in spite of attempts to make some of them scientifically precise, these words have all travelled the same path. From neutrality to hurt, ridicule, shame. They've all become a one word summing up: you are stupid, you are not like me, not like us. You don't belong.

■ ■ ■

IN SEPTEMBER, JESSICA e-mails me:

> Dear Judy,
>   We have been thinking to invite you to visit while we are in Taiwan. If you are interested, we can make a plan. Maybe Madelyne would like to go, too?
>   Jessica

■ ■ ■

FRIDAY AFTERNOON. GRACE is in front of her computer, scrolling through some of her favourite Sailor Moon sites. Jessica brings in a thermos of tea and pours a cup for me and one for herself. She sits down at the end of the table.

"David is already in Taiwan to see his father." She smiles and takes sip of tea. "He took some copies of Grace's book with him." Another sip. "He will give one to his father," she says.

At the other end of the table, Grace groans. "Jeez," she mutters to her screen.

Jessica ignores her. "David hasn't seen his father for six years."

AN EARLY EVENING in mid-November. Our flight to Taipei scheduled to leave any minute. Madelyne and I have scored some roomy seats just behind a bulkhead. As we settle into our seats, arranging our small pillows in the hope that we'll be able to sleep, the snow begins to fall. And fall and fall.

The crew, young Asian women and men, chatter in the galley area just in front of us as we wait for the de-icing crew to arrive and hose down the plane. Time slides into some unmarked zone where minutes sag into hours. Finally, just after midnight, there's an abrupt announcement. The de-icing crews have gone home. Our flight will leave as soon as possible in the morning. Our arrival in Taipei, where Grace and her parents will meet us, will be delayed by hours.

When Madelyne and I finally arrive at the ultramodern Taipei airport, we walk along a bright and nearly empty hallway, stiff-legged and groggy. In the enormous and eerily quiet baggage area, I glance around, wondering how we'll contact Grace and her parents if we miss them here. Abruptly, a short figure appears at the far end of the area. Grace. Waving both arms high above her head, she runs toward us.

"Over here! Here!" she shouts. We wave back, relieved to see her. In seconds Grace is in front of us. "Come!" she says. "Hurry! The train is going!"

Jessica catches up and bows. "Grace! Let Judy and Madelyne catch their breath." Jessica leads us toward the luggage carousel where bags are now tumbling onto the rotating belt. Grace slips her hand into mine as we walk.

"The train will leave very soon," she says in a low voice.

Jessica explains. "Because your plane was delayed, we make a small change in our plans. We will take the train now to Tainan and tomorrow we will visit David's father."

"No!" Grace's voice is loud. "I don't want to see him."

"Grace!" Jessica turns to her daughter. "He is your grand-father!"

JESSICA FINDS A taxi to take us to the train station. As we begin the short drive through Taipei, Grace leans her head against my shoulder. "He said Down," she says in a low voice close to my ear. In spite of my jetlag, I realize that Grace's grandfather, if he wants forgiveness for his words, faces a tough uphill battle with Grace.

A few hours later, an efficient train delivers us to Tainan in the south, a city facing the Taiwan Strait. Across the grey-blue water, Jessica says, is China. We check into the small hotel Jessica and David booked for us. They will stay with Grace in a townhouse a few blocks away.

That night, I sleep fitfully. At three I'm fully awake and finally fall into a light sleep just before my alarm goes off at seven. I wander down to the main floor of the hotel to an almost empty restaurant. Madelyne hasn't appeared yet. I stumble past the breakfast buffet, several long tables of food, recognizing almost nothing. A few bamboo baskets of steamed dumplings, something dark green that could be sautéed spinach. The other dishes, steaming and attractively arranged, are a mystery. And there's nothing that looks like coffee. With a fleeting stab of clarity, I realize I have a serious problem.

I ask the young waiter behind the tables if it's possible to get a cup of coffee. He looks at me blankly. I don't know a word of Mandarin. He points to a large urn at the centre of the buffet, which I've already determined holds green tea. Something I like well enough, in the afternoon or evening. I repeat, "Coffee?" wondering if I've become one of those tourists I mocked when I was young—someone who can't function unless everything is just like it is at home. Finally, I begin to fill my plate, a small mound of steamed greens, something black that could be seaweed sprinkled with sesame seeds, and a pale fleshy rectangle I decide is fish. I find a small table near the window, and just as I'm contemplating what to try first, the same young waiter appears, a small stainless steel pot in one hand, cup in the other.

"Coff-eee," he says, pouring the beautiful liquid into the cup. The weakest, most watered down coffee imaginable. I gulp it down and refill my cup. Quantity will have to replace quality. I begin to perk up as I feel a faint and comforting caffeine buzz.

A SHORT TIME later, David drops Grace, Jessica, Madelyne, and me in the centre of one of Tainan's shopping areas. It's still early, just past nine, and Jessica suggests we stop for a traditional Taiwanese breakfast snack, leading us to a small open café. It's cold, our breaths jabbing out in front of us. We find a table near the back of the café, where it's moist and warm. A few feet away, a huge vat of soy milk bubbles, wafting fragrant steam through the café.

"They serve a famous breakfast snack here," Jessica says. "People eat it on the way to work." Within minutes, wide bowls of steaming soy milk arrive, with a platter of thick, crunchy, deep-fried, foot-long sticks. I pick one up and take a bite. Delicious. My resolution to eat healthy food on this trip instantly vanishes.

"It's called *you tiao*," says Grace, flakes of her stick stuck to her lips. I nod, and for a moment, we all munch in the humid warmth of the café.

Jessica lifts her steaming bowl of soy milk and takes a sip. "Tonight," she says, as she sets down her bowl, "we've arranged to visit David's father."

Grace groans. "No!"

"Grace! He is your grandfather." Jessica looks at me over Grace's head, and I think I see a flicker of apprehension pass across her face.

"When was the last time you saw him?" I ask.

"David has not seen his father for six years. And Grace and I—" She pauses. "Grace refuses to see him. But now—"

She doesn't add what I think she'd like to say. That now they have something to show David's father; something that might convince him he was wrong about Grace.

Grace puts her bowl down. "I don't want to see him." Her voice rises over the hubbub of the café.

"Grace!" Jessica hisses, "not polite!"

"Yeah, yeah," Grace mutters, turning her head away from her mother and staring out the open front of the café.

That night, despite her protests, Grace is in the back seat of the car between Madelyne and me as we drive through block after block of low-rise industrial buildings enclosed by high chain-link fences. It's a moonless night, so dark I can only make out the shadowy shapes of the buildings as we drive past. David turns a corner and slows as he pulls the car up to double-wide chain-link fences. Behind the fence, I can make out a very large house and, nearby, more industrial-looking buildings.

"My father live here," David says, as he opens his door and unlocks the gates. Frenzied barking erupts. I feel Grace press against me as if she wants to hide from the sound. David pulls the car ahead and stops by what looks like a small, empty gatehouse. A motion-sensor light flicks on, flooding the area with a harsh brilliance. Three dogs, muscular and stocky, a breed I don't recognize, snarl and snap, as if they'd like to rip us apart. Taut chains pull them up just short of the car. David opens his door, says a few words in Mandarin, and like magic the dogs slink back to the shadows of the gatehouse. Jessica steps out of the car, and I'm about to open my door when Grace presses her head against my shoulder. "Don't go," she says. "I don't want to see him." Her voice quiet, urgent.

I glance at the house, an imposing three-storey residence with wide, graceful steps leading up to double doors. "But we've come all this way to give your grandfather your book."

"I don't want to see him." Grace's head presses firmly against my shoulder, as if she hopes to pin me in the car. "He said Down. To my face!" Her fingers twist in her lap.

The others are now all outside the car, waiting. "Grace, I want to meet your grandfather and see what he thinks about your book. Let's go together, okay?" I reach for the door handle.

Reluctantly Grace unpins my shoulder. "Okay. But no hugs!"

Inside, we find ourselves in a formal entrance hall dominated by a large ancestral shrine. A framed photo of an elderly woman sits on one side. "David's mother," whispers Jessica. We climb a couple of marble steps into a modern living room—black leather sofa and chairs; chrome and glass coffee table. An elderly man, bent and frail-looking, stands beside a woman who must be David's sister. David and Jessica smile and bow, and there's a rush of words in Mandarin. David turns to Madelyne and me and introduces us, and his father and sister bow from the waist. I bow in return, trying to mimic their movement, wondering if I look as awkward as I feel. We all sit down, and for a few moments, there's an uneasy silence as Grace's grandfather peers across the coffee table at us. Grace, wedged again between Madelyne and me, presses tight against my side, as if she'd like to disappear behind me.

David hands a copy of Grace's book to his father, saying something in Mandarin. I try to read the father's face, but all I can see is that he listens intently as his son talks, his eyes moving from Grace to me and back to Grace.

With unsteady hands the old man opens the book and slowly turns the pages. The silence stretches out. Jessica watches her father-in-law with an unreadable face, and David stares at the floor. Grace presses herself even tighter against me, her body tense. I take her small hand and squeeze it.

Finally, Grace's grandfather looks up. He slowly reaches a shaky hand across the coffee table to Grace. He says a few words and Jessica murmurs, "He says, 'Well done, Grace.'" David and Jessica both turn toward their daughter with the same expectant look. Grace presses her face harder into my shoulder. "No!" she says, her voice muffled in my sleeve. "He said Down!"

"Grace!" Jessica hisses, "it is not polite!"

Grace doesn't budge, her small face still pressed hard against me. The moment stretches out. David's father drops his hand and looks down. Beside him, David begins to talk, his voice low, compelling. I don't understand what he's saying, but I hear a tone I think I understand—please give her some time, let her come around. As David speaks, his father nods slowly, as if he's trying to make sense of something very complicated.

In the silence that follows, Jessica pulls a DVD from her purse. A few days earlier, Grace had been interviewed by a Taiwan TV station. David slides the DVD into the player. A palpable sense of relief floods the room.

As the clip plays, Grace pulls her face away from my side and turns to the TV, unable to resist watching herself as she switches effortlessly from English to Mandarin and back. David's father watches with what seems like unguarded approval. When the short piece ends, he lifts his hands and claps enthusiastically, nodding at Jessica and David. He doesn't dare look at Grace, though I sense his applause is for her.

MADELYNE AND I return home to Vancouver before Grace and her parents. When they're back, Jessica calls me. She tells me that after Madelyne and I left Taiwan, Grace was interviewed by several Taiwanese newspapers and that she met with the mayor of Tainan. "This story, Grace and her book, it is quite popular," she adds.

"What about Grace's grandfather?" I ask. "Do you think he feels differently now?"

"We are not sure. He doesn't say very much. But he send a gift to Grace, like a small dowry." Jessica pauses. "When we gave him Grace's book, we want to say, 'Look what the child you wanted to put away has done.' But we don't say that. We know no other grandchild has written a book."

- - -

A FEW DAYS later, Jessica calls. "Judy, Community Living wants to write something about Grace and her book. They want to meet her to ask questions. Would you like to go too?"

The following week, we're in the offices of Community Living BC, a provincial agency that provides support and services to people with developmental disabilities. The young woman who will write the article for *The Citizen*, a bimonthly newsletter published by Community Living, wants to know how Grace came to write a book.

Grace answers her questions with a disarming directness. Yes, she likes writing. She writes every week. Is there another book planned? Yes, two. And maybe a play.

I describe how Grace and I met each week, how Grace had usually written a rough draft of the next chapter, and how I helped her revise that draft. Jessica fills in the details about Grace's book launch and the World Down Syndrome Congress.

On our way home, Jessica drives as Grace and I share the back seat ("Sit with me, please?" Grace had begged as I'd opened the front passenger door). As we drive up the Stanley Park causeway onto the Lions Gate Bridge, it feels as if we're emerging from a long green tunnel into a wide circle of light—today, a fine pale blue. I feel a sudden smack of joy. It's so strong, so visceral that I have trouble figuring out what's causing it. Maybe it's the rare experience of being chauffeured through the park onto the bridge. Or maybe it's knowing that no matter what the future brings or doesn't bring to Grace, she has her book. That nothing can diminish that or take it away from her.

Grace turns to me, almost bouncing in her seat. "I'm a famous writer now!"

I smile, but abruptly her face turns serious. "So where's the black limousine?"

I burst out laughing. What writer, including myself, hasn't fantasized about the perks of fame, like a black limousine?

"What's so funny?" Grace demands.

"I'm sorry," I say. "But the sad truth is that most writers never get to ride in a black limousine."

"Why not?"

"That's a good question." For a brief moment I think of saying something about how little our society values the arts and writing, but realize that won't be a satisfactory answer to Grace. "I don't really know."

"Oh." Grace leans her head against my shoulder. "Can you find out?"

"I'll try," I say.

Grace slips her hand under my elbow. "Try hard, okay?"

■ ■ ■

NOT LONG AFTER the excitement of the book launch had subsided, Grace asked me if we could continue working together. I knew that she had some ideas for a second book—Cinderella-Grace goes into space—and that she'd started writing it. But when I asked her to send me some new writing, nothing arrived.

I also knew from the plays we'd seen together—*Cinderella: The Musical*, Shakespeare's *Romeo and Juliet*, and several of Kathleen's high school performances—that Grace loved theatre. A play seemed like it could be a natural follow-up to her book.

GRACE LIKED THE idea of a play. We met several times and talked about how to transform a chapter of her book into a scene on stage. But as we continued, I realized that a play was, in many ways, a demanding form. Stage directions needed to paint a brief but clear picture. Characters needed to show their thoughts and desires in words or action. Dialogue should be natural but revealing.

Every time we met, Grace and I talked about these ideas and how she could make them work. But when she sent me some new writing, I realized that what Grace really wanted to write was a big-budget movie, complete with all the special effects and gadgets she could conjure up. And that I was secretly hoping, as I had before we met the first time, that she would write a simple play telling her own story.

I began to cast about for a structure that would keep Grace grounded in reality. Many times over the months we'd worked together, Grace had asked me to watch her karate class. "Come!" she'd said. "I can show you my moves." It seemed her class was always at a time that was difficult for me. But as I thought about it, I wondered if karate could provide the bones of her play.

One Friday afternoon as we'd struggled through more discussion about how to build a play, Grace hopped up from her chair. "I want to show you something, okay?"

Just as I was about to stand up, Grace snapped a straight-armed punch into the air above my head. "That's one of the moves," she said. "My karate moves."

"How many moves are there?"

"Twenty-one. Want to see?"

I nodded. Grace stepped back from the table and turned to face the living room wall. She bowed deeply, launching into a series of kicks, punches, and lunges. I saw a fierce concentration on her face as she moved from one stance to the next.

Later I learned that this series of linked moves is called a *kata*. It must be performed smoothly, without breaks or hesitation, to move up to the next belt. Grace currently held a white belt, the first level, and if she could perform her *kata* as required, she would move up to a yellow belt.

As Grace finished, she bowed deeply to the wall and turned to me. "That bow was to the teacher. My master."

"It must be hard to remember all the moves."

Grace shrugged. "Not really." She raised her fists in one of the poses. "My mom says I spend too much time on it. I should work more on my writing. Blah, blah, blah." She giggled and glanced toward the kitchen, where Jessica sat at her computer.

"When is your karate class?"

"Mom! When's my class?"

Jessica popped her head out of the kitchen. "Thursdays at three thirty. Like always." She smiled at me, but her expression changed as she looked at her daughter. "Blah, blah, blah is not polite, Grace."

For the briefest moment, Grace looked contrite. "Sorry, Mom."

■ ■ ■

A WEEK LATER, I find myself in the hall adjoining Grace's church. A wide, high-ceilinged space that serves as a daycare during the week, a tea room on Sundays, and a home to many community activities. Years ago, my sons attended Cubs and Scouts here, wild evenings with boys careening around the gym until the leader called them in, and the boys, hair sweat-matted, cheeks red, slumped in a lopsided circle on the floor around him.

No longer dull and scratched, the wooden floor gleams like smooth, dark ice. New maroon velvet curtains enhance the stage where the boys performed skits that featured, without fail, body parts and noises. The high windows that line one wall, once a cause of parental trepidation as the boys bashed soccer balls off the walls and each other, are covered with protective wire mesh.

Today, the gym is quiet, Grace's karate class, small: two black-haired brothers, one about twelve, the other about six; a chunky, middle-aged woman who wins my immediate admiration for giving this a try; and Grace, looking smaller than usual in her too-large white uniform, with its rolled-up sleeves and legs. The teacher is a man about my age, grey-haired but very fit-looking. I'm sure I've met him before and I realize, after a few moments, that his son was one of the careening Scouts I remember. Grace sees me and gives a hop of excitement. Perched on the edge of the stage, my legs dangling, I wave at her. Some part of me longs to hop down and join her. But I stay put, suddenly feeling like the kid who's been asked to sit out in gym class.

Teacher stands in the middle of the gym, waiting silently as the class forms a ragged line in front of him. He bows deeply, and the class returns the bow, not in unison, but as a group that some day hopes to achieve unison. When the students straighten up, Teacher is silent for a moment. Abruptly he shouts, his strong voice filling the high spaces of the gym: "Right hand up! Kick!" The students step forward in a ragged line, arms punching forward, legs kicking high. "Left hand up! Kick!"

I study Grace's face. Her expression serious, she's concentrating with everything she's got.

The line moves slowly across the gym to the far wall, where the class turns and begins its return to the centre of the gym.

"Left knee up! Kick! Double kick! Face punch coming!"

From the sanctuary, the sounds of the choir practising for Sunday drift in: "In darkness and temptation, my light, my help is near."

As the students finish their warm-up, some practising punches and kicks, others windmilling their arms or flexing their shoulders, Teacher calls them in. "Time for attack," he announces. Small Brother yips with joy as Grace curls a fist, victory-style, toward herself. With his students crowding around him, Teacher asks, "Okay, who's first?" Grace's hand shoots up and she looks over to make sure I'm paying attention. Teacher nods as the class forms a loose circle around Grace.

"Enemies all around," Teacher yells.

Grace steps back as Middle-Aged Woman moves in.

"Face punch coming!" Teacher's voice bounces off the walls of the gym.

Middle-Aged Woman's fist shoots out perilously close to Grace's face. Grace raises an arm, meant to block the approaching fist, but her timing is off. In a real fight, Grace would have just taken a hard smack on the nose.

Another fragment of song leaks in from the sanctuary.

"Grace," Middle-Aged Woman says, her voice sounding loud and condescending, "you forgot to block."

Grace nods, her small face serious. They start again. Middle-Aged Woman's arm flies up, and this time, Grace lifts her arm, elbow out, just in time to perfectly block the attacking arm. I think I see Middle-Aged Woman scowl, but from this distance, I can't be sure.

"Enemies all around!" Teacher shouts. "I see someone

coming! Are you ready, Grace?" Middle-Aged Woman steps back as Small Brother moves closer. He jiggles a bright blue plastic shield almost as big as he is, taunting Grace to make a false move. She stands her ground and then lands a high kick squarely on the shield. Small Brother staggers back, but stays upright. He jiggles his shield again, and Grace steps toward him, readying for another high kick. Still jiggling, Small Brother retreats as his big brother moves in.

Big Brother, a handsome and serious boy, is the clear leader of the class, the one who executes moves with precision and a delicate balance. He wears a yellow belt, already a full level above Grace. I study his face. If any distaste or disapproval is likely to surface, surely it will be through him. Although Grace is more than twice his age, he probably sees her as smaller, weaker, someone who has to repeat things many times to get them, who talks with a thick tongue and doesn't always understand. But his face only reveals a high level of concentration. Grace stands in front of him, fists ready.

Teacher calls out again. "You have no friends! Everyone's an enemy! Attack!"

Grace lets fly a raised fist, punching close to Big Brother's face. He lifts an arm, blocking her. She punches again; he blocks once more. I see that they are, at this moment, evenly matched, both concentrating with all they've got.

After a few more moves, Teacher calls his class in around him. "Well done, Grace," he says. Grace glances over at me. I smile and give her a thumbs up. She hops up and down in front of Teacher.

"Grace." Teacher's voice is low, but his message clear: Stay focused. Her class once again forms a ragged line, Grace in the middle. Teacher faces his class and bows deeply. This time, almost in unison, the class bows deeply to Teacher.

And with that, the class is over.

Later, I'll read that a *kata* is more than the sum of its movements. There are layers of understanding, from the simplest, which is to focus on the position of the body in each movement, to the highest, where the student forgets all the previous layers and the *kata* performs itself. The point, I learn, is not to become better than others, but to become better than yourself.

The sounds of the choir drift in again as it repeats the hymn it's worked on for the entire class.

Grace skips over to me. "Did you like it? Want to join?"

I'm tempted to say yes. It would feel so good to block an opponent's move, to land a high kick. But this is Grace's class, not mine. "Maybe you can teach me some moves," I suggest.

"Okay," she says. "Stand up straight. I'll show you how to bow."

• • •

THE FOLLOWING WEEK, I ask Grace if she thinks she can use the structure of her *kata* in her play.

"What do you mean?" she asks.

"Well, your *kata* is twenty-one moves, right?" Grace nods.

"What if you used each move to tell part of the story?"

"You mean the students bow and it's like 'in the beginning'?"

"That's it! Want to give it a try?"

Grace nods, a slow, doubtful nod. I'm not sure myself how this could work, but I hope that jamming Grace's karate moves up against a new version of Cinderella will give her a structure and focus to hang on to.

What I don't mention is how the number twenty-one resonates in both Grace's *kata* and in the extra twenty-first chromosome embedded in every cell of her body.

PART FIVE

Me, as a Real Person

NOT LONG AFTER Grace and I began working on the idea of a play, I returned to New York with Jim to see Kathleen in her last student performance.

In a way, I was surprised to be there. Several times over the four years of her program Kathleen had called to tell me how unsure she was that she was doing the right thing. I thought about how she'd expressed it, from an early *It feels so competitive*, to *I've been out of my comfort zone since I got here*, and near the end of her second year, *I hate it here. I want to change programs*. This last year, whenever I'd asked how things were going, she'd replied with a flat *It's going*.

Every time Kathleen tried to talk to me about her doubts, I knew I could only dimly hear what she was trying to say. Part of me was thrown back to my own early doubts, to my regret that I didn't start writing when I was her age. When she called, often late at night, I'd sometimes launch into a monologue about how important it was not to give up, about how she needed to remember, to hold in her heart, some part of what had inspired her to want to act in the first place.

If she seemed willing to listen, I'd mention some of the roles she'd had. Remember Harriet, I'd say, shamelessly evoking her first role, the one I thought had hooked her on drama back in grade four. Or Viola in grade twelve? During one of the performances of *Twelfth Night* in the large auditorium at Kathleen's school, I'd sat near the back. Her drama teacher, in the row behind me, had leaned forward near the end of the play and whispered, *Have you ever seen such a Viola?* I hadn't, but then, I hadn't seen many Violas anywhere. But her words seemed to suggest that Kathleen had some talent, something I recalled when I tried to counter Kathleen's doubts.

As I talked, I recognized that what I was saying was coming as much from my own failure to follow my dream as it was from any understanding of Kathleen's dream and how it might be changing. Mostly she listened. Sometimes she humoured me by telling me I was good at pep talks. But we skirted around her concerns, never really facing them. In the end, she'd stuck with her program, deciding to postpone deciding about her future until after graduation.

THE MORNING AFTER Jim and I arrived for Kathleen's performance, as we returned to our small hotel in the East Village from a coffee run, Jim, checking his BlackBerry, tripped on the uneven sidewalk in front of a construction site. Like a slow-motion clip, he pitched forward, face down, his BlackBerry flying up in a graceful loop above his head.

I had no time to react, though he found a nanosecond to utter an uncharacteristic "Fuck!" just before his face smashed into the sidewalk with a sickening *thunk*. I bent down, almost afraid to look at him, as a young woman walking behind us rushed to help us. Jim staggered up, blood pouring from his cheek and nose. I bent down and found his glasses, the frame snapped but both lenses still intact. His BlackBerry was a few feet away, unharmed.

We stumbled to our hotel where the young doorman blanched as he held the door open. Within minutes, we were in a taxi on our way to the closest hospital, Beth Israel. Jim was quickly seen, scanned, and cleaned up by a friendly young doctor. As she dabbed a stinging antiseptic onto Jim's wounds, she grimaced. "Who knows what lives on our sidewalks."

That night, a patched-up Jim and I arrived at the studio where Kathleen's play would be performed. The young woman checking tickets, one of Kathleen's classmates, looked up at Jim, momentarily speechless as she struggled with whether to be horrified or admiring. Recovering, she blurted out, "Wow! Did you win?" We laughed and I explained the fall, not wanting to leave the impression that Kathleen had a brawling father who lost his bouts.

IN THIS LAST play, Kathleen was cast as the maid Catherine in David Mamet's Victorian comedy, *Boston Marriage*. Near the end of the first act, she timidly ventured onstage for the first time. "Excuse me, mum," she said in a voice I'd never heard her use, soft and deferential, with a subdued musical lilt. Her mistresses, two aging lesbians caught up in a desperate attempt to secure financial support and seduce the young girl one of them has fallen for, completely ignored her.

"Excuse me, mum," Kathleen repeated, in a louder but still deferential tone. Her mistresses didn't see or hear her. Kathleen tried several more times to deliver her message that the stove was broken and cook was leaving, until finally she was driven to shout: "Cook says you can kiss her arse goodbye!"

Although performed entirely by students, the verbal fireworks of Mamet's language sparked on stage. The characters Anna and Claire, long-time lovers, played by two of Kathleen's classmates, threw words like poisoned darts at each other. They never addressed their maid, Catherine, by her own name, accusing her of being one of the idiot Irish poor—"Don't you know that crop rotation could have prevented the potato famine?"

Catherine stood by, cowed, or so it seemed, as her life fell apart both on and off stage. Her fellow had abandoned her, and she might be pregnant and ruined, though late in the play, she offered, with a sly hint of how much she'd been suppressing, "We like to do it up against a tree, mum."

THE NEXT MORNING, over a late breakfast, Kathleen told me (Jim was still groggy from the pain medication he'd been taking and had decided to stay in our hotel room) how terrified she'd been every time she came out on stage, knowing she had to speak with a Scottish lilt and that a few theatrical agents were rumoured to be in the audience.

"How do you feel now?" I asked.

Kathleen stared back at me. She had dark circles under her eyes, her face pale. "I don't know." She picked at her food. "It's over now, so that's good. But I don't know." She looked away. "Remember I told you about going to see that play on Broadway a few weeks ago?"

I nodded. One of the benefits of Kathleen's program has been that she's been able to buy student-rate tickets to some of the best theatre in New York.

"When I saw that, I wanted to do that. To be up there on the stage." A small smile flicked across her face for a second. "But at school, they tell us over and over that most of us won't succeed. Most of us will never be working actors. So…"

At Kathleen's age, I'd had the same doubts. How could I ever make a living as a writer? I had no idea. I didn't know any writers, and at that time, the sixties, in the world that was visible to me, women writers seemed a rarity.

I took a sip of my now cool coffee. "But how will you know," I began, "unless you—"

"Mom. They're being realistic. So maybe I should, too."

I sat back, cradling my cup, unable to come up with a convincing response. Maybe Kathleen was right.

●●●

KATHLEEN'S DREAM TO become an actor had taken hold when she played Harriet the Hamburger in her grade four class. For several years, I'd attempted to capture in a short story what I'd felt as Kathleen had learned her role as Harriet and I was four hundred miles away with my parents during the final weeks of my mother's life. I wanted to distill how it felt as if the air had been sucked out of their apartment; how my father shuffled between anger and frustration with a wife who insisted on staying in bed all day, in the many moments when his memory failed him, and grief that seemed like a blow to his knees when he remembered that his wife of almost sixty years was dying. I wanted to capture the interruptions of Kathleen's calls, nightly reminders that her life, and mine, would carry on; how her insistence that I create a realistic talking hamburger hand puppet collided with the unrelenting details that told me that my mother's end was close.

I poked at my memories, trying to find the places where what had really happened could be pushed, exaggerated, transformed into fiction. My brother John became a chain-smoking Jack, given to blunt words, while my father's one twist of my mother's quilt grew into a history of a physically abusive man. Kathleen became Jessie, a girl with long, dark hair and an emerging ability to mimic a jaded teen.

But every attempt I made felt like a weak version of what had really happened. Many times I was taken back to the moment when I couldn't bring myself to open the door to the Creative Writing Department, the moment when the weight of my mother's dream to be a writer washed over me and my own doubts welled up. That voice that had spoken then—*What makes you think you can be a writer?*—was still there, loud and clear. Maybe that door was never meant to be opened, I thought. Maybe I still had nothing to say.

ONE MORNING AFTER we'd returned from seeing Kathleen's last student play, I sat down to write. By now, I was at least aware, if not a regular devotee, of the "ass in chair" mantra I'd heard from successful writers. As I faced that intimidating blank screen, I suddenly thought of Harriet, feeling a surge of regret that she'd been cast into my ever-growing digital pile of cast-offs. *You,* she seemed to say, *why did you forget about me?*

You, I thought. You, the seldom-used, often awkward, distancing second-person point of view. The point of view Grace and I had skipped over when we'd talked about POV. The more I thought about it, the more *you* felt like a fresh way into the story, a way that would let me breath as I wrote. A fictionalized version of the story began to pour out.

Jack tilts his chair back, smoke drifting up from a saucer beside him. "Need a big purple job," he says. Kenny, your younger brother, slings a monster purple pill across the kitchen table. Jack slots it into a container. "Blood regulator," he says to you. "And some green gel caps, to ward off—" He sings his next word. "Con-sti-pa-tion." He picks up a small brown pill between his thumb and forefinger.

"These," he whispers, "are the real magic. Morphine." Jack's voice flattens. "Two now. One more than last week." He takes a drag, exhales a perfect circle.

Kenny's meaty hand swats it away. "Christ," *he says,* "she hates that."

Just as I'd witnessed when Grace wrote the scene on the deck of the *Titanic*—and she seemed to be on the deck of the ship as she wrote—I abruptly found myself back in the kitchen of my parents' apartment, talking with my fiction-alized brothers in a way we never had in real life. As night fell in my story, we sat together, sorting my mother's over-whelming array of pills.

Pill-sorting again. As Jack pushes a mound of big purple ones toward you, the phone rings. It's your eight-year-old daughter, Jessie.

"Mum, Mum." Your cue to pay close attention. *"I got the lead. I'm Harriet!"*

"Great!"

"Mum." There's no faking with this girl. *"The play my class is doing.* Harriet the Hamburger.*"

"You're a hamburger?"

Jack lifts an eyebrow at Kenny.

Jessie's already mastered jaded teenager. "Mum. It's about the human digestive system. I get eaten and then—"

"Is this a speaking part?"

"Mum. I talk all the way to the end."

You wince.

"You have to make Harriet. So she can fit on my hand and talk."

"Like a real talking hamburger," you say. *Almost identical smiles flit across your brothers' faces.*

As I wrote, I could hear my father shuffle into the kitch-en and set the kettle on the stove with a clink. I saw myself walk into the bedroom my mother hadn't left in days.

You sit on a chair pulled up to the side of your mother's bed, holding her hand, bony and cool now. You talk in a soft voice, tell her about pill-sorting at night with Jack and Kenny, about Jessie and her phone calls, about Harriet.

I wrote as fast as I could, pushing my memories around even more. I gave Jack a disdain for gays; Kenny a good Scout persona, a soft belly, and a tendency to cry easily. My fictional father and Jack had a troubled history. Every night, my brothers and I (I was now Lenore) sat in the kitchen and sorted pills. Late one night in that bleak fictional kitchen, we lost it.

Advanced pill-sorting. Your brothers now trust you with two mounds. Green gel caps and yellow minis. You push your mounds into lines, green-yellow-green, play with them like beads. Jack goes to the fridge and takes out six Kokanees, landing them like a six-pack in the middle of the table. He pulls a bottle opener from his vest and starts uncapping. "Glass?" You shake your head, take a brown bottle, and the three of you clink together.

"Fuck," says Kenny. "What is the point?" He flicks a few pills across the table. Jack stares at his beer, picking the label, his face unreadable. Then he glances up with that look that never failed to grab you as a girl. Eyes bright, glistening almost, mouth slightly open, ready. A look that says anything can happen now. He glances at you, at Kenny, and starts to fire pills across the room. Kenny grins. Bends his head and flicks a curved finger. You join in. Pills ping off the stove, the fridge, a hailstorm of high-priced Smarties.

In seconds, it's over. Kenny squeezes his eyes shut and tears roll down his cheeks. You start to stand when he opens his eyes and you see he's laughing. Jack fishes in his pocket and pulls out a rumpled Kleenex. "Here," he says, shoving it at Kenny, "wipe the snot, man."

FOR SEVERAL DAYS, the end of the story eluded me. I didn't want to end with my mother's death or my trip back home. I needed something else, but I had no idea what it was. Then one day, in one of those moments that Margaret Atwood has described as "a lot of staring out the window," the final scene came to me.

Jessie, in her little-girl mode, jaded teenager cast aside for the moment, took my face and squeezed hard. "You look funny," I heard her say. She leaned in close. "You," she said, her dark eyes holding me, "you will live forever."

I wrote as fast as I could, before what I'd seen vanished. I knew I'd found a magical place, where I lived in my story for a few moments. And I knew too, that Jessie's words were the very words I wish I could have said to my mother in those last days.

That story, called "Pill-Sorting for Dummies," went on to place in a fiction contest run by one of Canada's oldest literary magazines, *Room*, and to be published in the magazine. To celebrate International Women's Day, *Room* hosted an evening of readings at Joy Kogawa House in Vancouver. Along with the other winners of their fiction contest, I was invited to read my story to a packed, mostly female, audience. And as I read, it was as if my mother was beside me, listening. At the end of my reading, as the applause faded, the audience evaporated for a few seconds and it felt as if my mother and I were alone. She smiled and placed her hand against my cheek. *You're a writer,* I heard her say.

● ● ●

NOT LONG AFTER I suggested to Grace that she use the twenty-one moves of her karate *kata* as a structure for her play, she sent me the pages she'd written. As I read through them, I saw that she'd taken my suggestion to heart. Each scene began with a group of karate students wearing their Shotokan karate uniforms performing one of the moves of Grace's *kata*.

The students kneel down on the ground without using their hands. But Grace's attempt felt like two unconnected ideas hobbled together, karate moves smashed up against a fairy tale. I knew there was a connection between the discipline and dignity of the *kata*, with its idea of the karate student striving to be a better version of herself, and the story of the mistreated girl who's finally revealed to be worthy of a prince's love.

And I thought about Grace's own story, how it resonated in both her *kata* and the classic Cinderella story. It was as if Down syndrome was a disguise that hid Grace's real self as well as Cinderella's rags hid hers. The cloak of Down syndrome presented Grace as slow, dull, with an expectation of unrelenting cheerfulness. Her real self was smart, sensitive, aware. And cheerful when she had a reason to be cheerful.

But how, I wondered, to capture this in a play? And how could Grace capture this in her writing? I began to think that I'd set up an impossible expectation for her.

ANYONE WHO READS about mental disability will sooner or later stumble across a short personal essay called "Welcome to Holland." Thirteen years after her son, Jason, was born with Down syndrome, Emily Perl Kingsley, a writer with *Sesame Street,* wrote the following:

I am often asked to describe the experience of raising a child with a disability—to try to help people who have not shared that unique experience to understand it, to imagine how it would feel. It's like this...

When you're going to have a baby, it's like planning a fabulous vacation trip—to Italy. You buy a bunch of guidebooks and make your wonderful plans. The Coliseum. The Michelangelo David. The gondolas in Venice. You may learn some handy phrases in Italian. It's all very exciting.

After months of eager anticipation, the day finally arrives. You pack your bags and off you go. Several hours later, the plane lands. The stewardess comes in and says, "Welcome to Holland."

"Holland?!?" you say. "What do you mean Holland?? I signed up for Italy! I'm supposed to be in Italy. All my life I've dreamed of going to Italy."

But there's been a change in the flight plan. They've landed in Holland and there you must stay.

The important thing is that they haven't taken you to a horrible, disgusting, filthy place, full of pestilence, famine, and disease. It's just a different place.

So you must go out and buy new guidebooks. And you must learn a whole new language. And you will meet a whole new group of people you would never have met.

It's just a different place. It's slower-paced than Italy, less flashy than Italy. But after you've been there for a while and you catch your breath, you look around...and you begin to notice that Holland has windmills...and Holland has tulips. Holland even has Rembrandts.

But everyone you know is busy coming and going from Italy...and they're all bragging about what a wonderful time they had there. And for the rest of your life, you will say, "Yes, that's where I was supposed to go. That's what I had planned."

And the pain of that will never, ever, ever, ever go away
…because the loss of that dream is a very very significant
loss.

But…if you spend your life mourning the fact that
you didn't get to Italy, you may never be free to enjoy the
very special, the very lovely things…about Holland.

The doctor who delivered Jason told his parents he would
never walk or talk; that they should put him in an institution. But they brought their son home and began an intense program of stimulation. By the time he was six, Jason
was reading at a level above many of his "normal" peers and
could do simple math. Emily Perl Kingsley and her son
began to give lectures to parents and medical personnel. As
Andrew Solomon notes in *Far from the Tree*, his astonishing
and moving book about how parents accept the children
they never wanted, the children they never hoped to have,
Emily Perl Kingsley felt she had mastered DS. With a friend
who also had Down syndrome, Jason co-authored a book,
Count Us In. He was profiled on national TV and appeared
on *Sesame Street*. He was, Solomon writes, the first celebrity
with Down syndrome.

But as Jason grew older, things began to unravel. He held
onto his interest in TV shows and toys intended for much
younger children. In his soccer games, he sometimes forgot
which team he was on. He wasn't invited to parties with his
classmates. A couple of jobs after high school ended in Jason
being fired for doing things his own way.

It was around this time that his mother Emily wrote,
"Welcome to Holland." She'd taken a son whom she'd been
told would never do anything, who wouldn't talk or even
recognize her, and had shown the world what he could do.
But she wondered if his achievements were really more for

her own satisfaction than Jason's happiness.

She realized that as high achieving as Jason was, he'd never be able to do many things that the non-disabled take for granted. He was too bright for many others with Down syndrome, but not bright enough for non-disabled people. Jason was in a lonely spot, his mother said, a place where he was without peers.

AS I READ about Jason Kingsley, I recognize similarities with Grace's story. Her high functioning, her ability to read and write, her learning another language, her very awareness of how the world views her—all these set her apart from many others with Down syndrome. She is in the same lonely place as Jason Kingsley. A place where her abilities not only separate her but can raise unrealistic expectations.

And I am one of the guilty parties. *Write a play,* I'd said, *and find some creative way to combine the seemingly unconnected—karate, Cinderella, you. You wrote a book, you can do this, too.* As I think about this, I cringe. My expectations about what Grace can do, the places she can go in her writing, are very unrealistic. I doubt that many writers, myself included, could do what I've suggested that Grace do.

• • •

THE LONELINESS THAT Jason Kingsley and Grace have experienced is something I hadn't seen when I met Russell Morfitt, the young man who works in a large grocery store and lives in his own apartment. I decide to return to Victoria to see if I can find out how Russell, who's also very high functioning, has apparently managed to escape loneliness.

When I call Russell's mother, Peggy, to arrange a visit, she laughs when I ask about friends.

"I call Russell and his friends the gang of four," she says. "They're always doing things together."

The following Saturday morning, after a two-hour ferry ride from the mainland, I arrive at the Morfitt house. Peggy, a confident woman in her seventies, and her husband, George, a former provincial auditor-general, meet me at their door. "Come in, come in!" Peggy says. "They're all here, ready to go." As Peggy ushers me into the adjoining family room, I hear a burst of laughter float above a hubbub of talk. Here I find Russell and his close friends Susan, Cindy, and Scott, as well as some of their mothers.

Susan Anthony, forty-two, is one of Russell's oldest friends. A short, round-faced woman with a warm smile, Susan works at Old Navy. "I clean there," she says, "four hours, four days each week." Sue tells me she has a cleaning cart with a large mop that she pushes through the store and that she picks up clothes as well. She's worked at Old Navy for the past seven years. "They're completely accepting of me," Sue says. "They don't treat me different."

Lately, Sue has been off work for about a month because of pains in her legs. Her manager came to visit her, and Sue was afraid she was going to be fired. Instead, he brought cards and stuffed animals from her fellow employees.

Has she ever been bullied or teased, I ask? Sue nods. "In elementary school, there was the odd student. My best friend, she had Down syndrome, too. She would get more teasing than me. So I had to stick up for her. If they didn't stop, I'd go to the teacher or sometimes the principal. We knew our rights, that we had to be respected, so I would speak up." A look of sadness passes over her face. "My friend died when she was twenty."

Nine years ago, Sue moved into an apartment with Cindy. "We met in Special Olympics," she says, "and just hit it off. Living with Cindy is a luxury. We take turns cooking and we divide up the cleaning. Sometimes we have our moments, but they don't last long." The apartment Sue and Cindy share is in a building where several apartments are operated by Community Living of Victoria, a private organization that also provides assistance with shopping, appointments, and banking.

I ask Susan how she'd like others to see her. She doesn't hesitate. "See who I am, not what I am."

Sue's mother, Lorna Anthony, is equally clear when I ask her if she thinks inclusion is a reality now. "Yes, I think so," she says, "I don't feel Sue has ever been excluded—if anything, she's had it easier than some people with a disability who look normal."

Lorna adds, "When Sue was born, my husband went to see the public health officer, and he said, 'Well, of all the disabilities, you sure picked the worst one,' and gave him a brochure called 'The Mongoloid Baby.' I went to the library, but very little had been written. Eventually, I found a book called *David*. It was mainly a black-and-white picture book. It changed my life, that book.

"And in the building we lived in then, our neighbours rallied around us and we became very close." She smiles. "For Sue's fortieth birthday, we rented a hall and about one hundred and twenty people came, including some of those first neighbours."

Sue's roommate, Cindy Burdett, is thirty-eight. She has fine features, glasses, and a trim pageboy cut. Like Sue, she has an open, friendly face. Cindy's worked at Starbucks for six years. "I work three days a week," she says, "cleaning, taking out garbage, cleaning out the bathrooms, filling up the milk and creamers and the sugar." And she has a second job at Royal LePage. "My father had the job, but he had heart problems, so he gave it to me."

Cindy tries to tell me what her job there involves, but her speech is difficult to understand.

Cindy is active in sports—swimming and golf—and confides that she and Russell swim together. "Russell and me, now we're engaged. We've been together ten or eleven years."

I ask Cindy if she and Russell are thinking of getting married. "No." Her quick and very definite reply surprises me. "My father told me, if I get married, I have to move in with Russell. And leave Susan."

"And you and Susan," I suggest, "are happy together."

Cindy grins. "Perfect match!"

Scott Jones is the third member of "the gang of four." Although he's forty-three, he has a soft, rounded face that makes him look younger than he is. He's an attractive man, with the same friendly look as his friends. Scott has two jobs. Like Russell, he works at Thrifty's, keeping the produce bins clean and full. He also works one day a week at the Uplands Golf Club, cleaning clubs, driving golf carts, and generally helping out. "Right now," Scott tells me, "golf is my life." He's been at the club for ten years. "I love it there, my boss, Don, is the best boss. I can always crack a joke with him." Scott smiles. "And I'm the best golfer. I have two holes in one."

When I talk to Scott's mother, Janet, later, she confirms what Scott says. "He can hit over two hundred yards." She laughs. "He's better than I am. And when there's a tournament, the club pro asks Scott to hit the first ball."

Scott's dream, he says, is "to have my own business selling autographed pictures. I want to be successful. If I want to give it a try," he adds, softly, as if repeating something he's heard many times, "that's okay."

Janet shakes her head when she recalls Scott's early days. "Scott was born seven weeks early and was very sick. He wasn't supposed to live. When he was a year old, we couldn't believe he was still around." She pauses. "People around us were thinking long term, that we should institutionalize him. We said no. My husband was in the military, as a dentist, so we decided to go to Germany." Janet smiles. "We've had twenty-one moves with Scott. We were in Washington D.C. at the time Rose Kennedy was doing her wonderful work with the Special Olympics. While we were there, I was asked to join a group called Mothers of Young Mongoloids. I couldn't believe it. But I went and the name eventually did change."

Does she think Scott has been included? Janet doesn't hesitate. "I think he's really included. He can be a real goof, of course, and I feel he depends on Susan a lot—they talk every day. But he's more independent now." Scott still lives in his parents' basement. "I'm sixty-eight and my husband is seventy," Janet says. "We'd like Scott to go into a Community Living apartment like Susan and Cindy, but there's no room. He had a chance several years ago, but he didn't want to do it." Unspoken is the concern of all parents like Janet.

Where will their son or daughter live when they're no longer here? Who will take over the responsibility? It's something I know Grace's parents also worry about.

"Scott's had an unbelievable life. He's been spoiled rotten." Janet smiles again, taking any sting out of her words. "What I mean is, he's been very fortunate."

Scott echoes his mother's words. "If someone is a Down syndrome, that's okay," he says, adding, "Since I was a little kid, I was always a happy guy. I feel like a very special kind of guy."

At thirty-five, Russell is the youngest of his gang. He wears glasses and is a fine-featured, good-looking young man. Today, he's wearing grey dress pants and a navy blazer. Not sure if he'll remember me, I remind him about our previous meeting, but he cuts me off. "I remember meeting you," he says.

"So how are things now?" I ask. "Any changes?"

RUSSELL TELLS ME he's still working three days a week at Thrifty's ("I adore them, they rock," he says when I ask if he still likes it there) and living in his own apartment. "My brother moved out and I moved in," he says. "I find it free, good. Sometimes I make a mess, then clean it up, without people bugging me. And I do my own cooking—Ichiban noodles for lunch sometimes and order in for dinner. Pizza. Weight Watchers. And I use the microwave."

I ask him about his girlfriend, Cindy. Russell leans forward in his chair across from me. "Cindy is my hot fox, my hot mama." He grins, adding, "The world says, *oo, ick, ick.* Scott says, 'Barfarama!' He thinks I'm too mushy." But Russell clearly doesn't agree. And marriage? "Not yet," he says, "we're still on a holding pattern, we have to learn to cope, to really get along"—he pauses—"and clean windows."

When I ask Russell about his hopes for the future, he tells me he wants to be one of those actors on the *Comedy Hour,* like Jerry Seinfeld. "In school they thought I was funny. But I like Kramer best," he confides.

I recall Russell's reaction to the word *Down* at our first meeting. "Don't say Down," he'd urged me with the same intense distaste I'd seen in Grace. I ask him how he feels now about that word. Russell takes a moment before answering. "I don't look like the person," he says. "Sometimes people put bad information in my skull. They don't see me for who I really am." He leans forward. "That's not what I see in the mirror."

"What do you see?" I ask.

Russell smiles as he leans back in his chair. "I see attractive, funny, really good-looking, normal, suave, dashing." He says this in his straightforward way, without a hint of arrogance or superiority.

"And are you happy?"

He almost scoffs. "Of course I'm happy. I love people. The world is great to live in. I love to live in this place. I want peace. Everything's sparkly. I want people to be happy."

WHEN I'VE FINISHED meeting with the "gang of four," I stand in the Morfitts' kitchen as Russell and his friends noisily pull on their coats and shoes. They're taking the bus to Russell's place, where they plan to watch a movie and order in. The area near the Morfitts' back door fills up with an excited buzz.

"What bus are we taking?" Cindy asks.

"Come on, let's go," Scott urges.

As they file out the door, Peggy claps her hand on her son's broad back. "Follow this one," she says. "He knows where he's going."

IN THE SUDDEN quiet of the Morfitt kitchen, I ask Peggy and George if they think we live in an inclusive society. There's a long pause. "I don't think so," George says, "although it's getting better."

Peggy adds, "People in contact one on one, there's no problems. It's getting past that stereotype. TV helps, shows like *Life Goes On,* movies." She pauses, adding, "When Russell was little, friends sent me articles—skull reconstruction, tongue surgery. But being a schoolteacher, I've gone the enrichment route. You get what you expect. Aim high, you can always adjust after."

George hints at the same lonely place of high functioning that I've seen with Grace. "We didn't put Russell in Special Olympics at first. We didn't think he was ready to mix with others with Down syndrome—a lot of them are not as quick as he is. But he met Susan, and she's very verbal." Peggy adds, "And he found Cindy about ten years ago."

I know from my earlier visit that it hasn't been easy for them to arrive where they are now. "He's fought the stereotype all the way," Peggy has told me. Now, as I pull on my coat, she laughs. "I always say, Russell's a Morfitt before he's anyone with Down syndrome."

I think of what Scott's mother, Janet, had told me when we talked. "It's a wonderful group of friends. They're very natural, they can bicker, be goofy—" She'd stopped, and I thought I'd seen her eyes fill. "It truly is unbelievable."

In the late afternoon, after I've said goodbye, I take the ferry back to Vancouver. Once we've pulled out of the harbour, I walk outside to the deck. A crisp gust of wind catches me, making me lean forward as I make my way to the railing. It's a clear fall day, the sky blue and cloudless. I rest my hands on the railing, thinking about what Russell has: parents who've supported and fought for him over the years, a tight group of friends who love to be together, a job that he loves, a safe and independent place to live. A life, I think.

How Grace would love to have that. And she does have some of it—the supportive parents, a safe home. But the rest—a job she loves, a close group of friends—so far, has eluded her.

• • •

THE GREAT MAJORITY of expectant parents who are told they will likely have a baby with Down syndrome choose to abort it. In every developed country, the rate of abortion of Down syndrome fetuses is very high—over 90 percent in many countries. That high rate has led to speculation that with even more accurate and less invasive prenatal testing, Down syndrome could be eliminated altogether one day.

Denmark is often cited as the country where this might first happen. In 2005, Denmark began a national screening program. By the following year, 93 percent of pregnant women were being screened and the number of live births of babies with Down syndrome was cut in half. That number has fallen by 13 percent every year since. Some scientists have predicted that by 2030 Denmark could be the first nation where no one is born with Down syndrome.

But even as testing and abortion become more widely available to all expectant mothers, people with Down syndrome are living much longer lives (in Canada and the U.S., the average life expectancy is forty-nine years). As a result, the actual number of people living with Down syndrome is rising and may even double in the next twenty-five years.

For many decades, there was almost no scientific interest in research into treatment of Down syndrome. The discovery of the cause in 1959 by the French scientist Jérôme Lejeune only highlighted the huge task involved—sifting through all five hundred or so genes on the twenty-first chromosome.

But in the 1980s a new model of the disorder changed everything. Over many years, Muriel Davisson, a researcher in Bar Harbor, Maine, developed a mouse with many of the characteristics of Down syndrome, including, amazingly, similar facial characteristics. The mouse model was given the catchy handle of Ts65Dn.

Enter Dr. Alberto Costa, a neuroscientist and father of a daughter with Down syndrome. When his daughter was born, Costa decided to devote his research to the study of Down syndrome. And Davisson's mouse was what he needed to do that. In 2007, Costa published a study that showed that one injection of memantine, a drug used to treat Alzheimer's, increased memory in the Down-like mice.

Other scientists have tested other drugs with equally startling results. For example, in 2009, at the University of California at San Diego, William C. Mobley conducted tests that showed that an increase of norepinephrine in the brains of these mice allowed them to learn as if they were normal mice. The next year, Paul Greengard at Rockefeller University showed similar results by lowering the levels of B-amyloid in the mice. Costa is currently conducting a clinical trial of memantine in young adults with Down syndrome.

Costa's approach represents a radical shift: treat Down syndrome, rather than detect and destroy it. Interviewed by the *New York Times,* Costa set out the stakes: "It's like we're in a race against the people who are promoting those early screening methods. These tests are going to be quite accessible. At that point, one would expect a precipitous drop in the rate of children born with Down syndrome. If we're not quick enough to offer alternatives, this field might collapse."

Costa believes that memantine works by normalizing how the brain cells of the Down mice use the neurotransmitter NMDA. People with Down syndrome have 50 percent more proteins encoded in their twenty-first chromosome. That, Costa thinks, makes their NMDA receptors hyperactive. Memantine reduces some of that hyperactivity, getting rid of some of the "noise" that interferes with normal reception.

It's an astounding turn of events. As Costa says, even ten years ago no one was thinking about drug therapies for people with Down syndrome. Now the race is for research dollars. However, Costa notes, many geneticists expect Down syndrome to disappear, so why fund research? And some parents of Down syndrome children also question whether treatment is the way to go. A recent survey in Canada found that 27 percent of those parents said they wouldn't want drug treatment for their child, and another 32 percent said they weren't sure.

Costa doesn't see it that way. He says this treatment is no different than treating any other disease or disability. And behind his work is a very personal goal: to help young people with Down syndrome, including his daughter, have a more independent life.

And a very recent development in Down syndrome research is even more startling than Costa's work. Researchers at the University of Massachusetts have demonstrated that they can "silence" one of the three copies of the twenty-first chromosome in cells taken from someone with Down syndrome.

The leader of the research team, Jeanne Lawrence, stated in *The Guardian,* "This will accelerate our understanding of the cellular defects in Down's syndrome and whether they can be treated with certain drugs. The long-range possibility—and it's an uncertain possibility—is a chromosome therapy for Down's syndrome. But that is ten years or more away. I don't want to get people's hopes up."

In spite of her caution, Lawrence's words do raise hopes that some of the more serious medical issues that can arise with Down syndrome will be able to be avoided or at least ameliorated in the future. At the same time, this research brings up the argument that's made by those who oppose the constant push for earlier and less invasive prenatal detection of Down syndrome: that Down syndrome is not a defect but is a normally occurring part of the human spectrum.

When I mentioned this research to Jessica, she told me that Grace had asked her brother Albert many times to "take out my extra chromosome." She smiled. "I told her that's impossible, because it's in every single cell," but she added, "I feel sympathy for her every time she says that."

● ● ●

OFTEN GRACE AND I met at Starbucks to spend an hour revising Grace's writing. I'd bring up the latest writing Grace had sent me on my laptop, and Grace would pull her chair close to mine, so we could begin going over her writing, word by word.

One afternoon, as we were about to leave, Grace looked up at me. "I want to show you something," she said. She pulled a yellow ribbon from her bag and held it up. "For bowling. I joined a team." The ribbon said "participant" and at the top were the words *Special Olympics*.

"Bowling! How do you like it?"

"It's lots of fun." Grace carefully placed the ribbon back in her bag. "I like my team."

EUNICE KENNEDY SHRIVER, the founder of the Special Olympics, had an older sister, Rosemary, who'd been born with mild mental disability. In her early twenties, Rosemary developed bouts of irritability and mood swings. At twenty-three, she had a frontal lobotomy, an operation her doctors felt would help calm her. But the result was even greater disability, and Rosemary was placed in an institution for the rest of her life.

Rosemary's mental capacities were a tightly held secret until 1962, when Shriver published an article in the *Saturday Evening Post*. At the time, people like Rosemary were considered by most to be beyond hope, dark and shameful offspring. Some parents, on learning that their baby was retarded (the word used then), immediately placed him or her in an institution, and filed a death notice in the local paper. "Out of sight" often became a lifetime sentence.

In her article, Shriver wrote bluntly that her sister was retarded. Such a statement, coming from a member of a wealthy established family, was an astounding admission.

After visiting some state institutions, Shriver described appalling conditions, and patients with nothing to do.

That year a woman called Shriver and told her she couldn't find a summer camp for her "retarded" son. No camp was willing to take him.

In an interview on National Public Radio years later, Shriver recalled that conversation. "I said: 'You don't have to talk about it anymore. You come here a month from today. I'll start my own camp. No charge to go into the camp, but you have to get your kid here, and you have to come and pick your kid up.'" With those few words, Shriver began what became known as Camp Shriver at her home in Maryland.

The first counsellors she hired to help with her camp, she recalled, were afraid the children would be hard to teach, maybe difficult to handle. (When I read this, I'm abruptly transported back to that time in the early sixties when I would have been a young teenager and felt the same, I know.) Shriver was clear in her article. There are major differences, she wrote, between the mentally ill and the mentally retarded. Most of the mentally retarded are emotionally stable. They do not go crazy, she said.

At the time Shriver started her camp, people with intellectual disabilities were thought to be incapable of taking part in play and recreation. A scientist at the University of Toronto, Dr. Frank Hayden, studied the effect of regular exercise on a group of intellectually disabled students at an inner school in Toronto. He found these students could become fit and take part in sports, and that it was lack of opportunity, not disability, that had stopped them. He proposed a national sport competition for intellectually disabled students.

Hayden's work came to the attention of Shriver, who had been directing the Joseph P. Kennedy Foundation for several years. And a young fitness instructor in Chicago, Anne Burke, wrote to the Kennedy Foundation proposing a one-time city-wide track meet for intellectually disabled youth, modelled on the Olympics. Shriver jumped on Hayden's and Burke's suggestions, and in 1968 she organized, with the financial backing of the Kennedy Foundation, the first International Special Olympics at Soldier Field in Chicago. One thousand athletes, mostly Americans, and twelve athletes from Dr. Hayden's school in Toronto took part.

Speaking to less than one hundred people scattered throughout the 85,000-seat stadium, Shriver addressed the athletes at the opening of the games. She evoked the memory of gladiators entering the arena in ancient Rome, and said the words that had inspired those gladiators so long ago:

Let me win.
But if I cannot win,
Let me be brave
In the attempt.

The press took almost no notice, but Mayor Richard Daley of Chicago, standing beside Shriver that day, predicted that the event would have a far-reaching effect. And he was right. Shriver's words became the motto of the Special Olympics. Now a worldwide organization with over three million intellectually disabled athletes participating, the Special Olympics runs national and international events, and also supports local teams through weekly practices.

The Special Olympics has been criticized for segregating, and therefore marginalizing, the very individuals it supports. But it's impossible to argue that the non-intellectually disabled world, the "normal" world, as we often think of it, encourages those like Grace to sign up for her local sports team. The story of Sadie Gates, of Vancouver, illustrates the point.

Sadie, eleven, wanted to join a girls' soccer team. So in 2007, her mom, Abbe, signed her up, buying her cleats and a new ball. When Sadie showed up for the first practice, the coach took her mom aside and told her Sadie was welcome at practices, but she would not be allowed to play in any games. Her Down syndrome made her a liability to the team.

Abbe Gates left that practice in tears, but she didn't give up on her daughter's passion for soccer. Instead, the following spring, she started a team called the Blazing Soccer Dogs for children with and without intellectual disabilities. The team has thrived and has added a younger division called the Soccer Pups. But it's a team where everyone who signs up knows it plays by different rules: difference is welcome, and winning does not trump everything else.

● ● ●

AT THE STARBUCKS where Grace and I often met, a middle-aged woman sometimes took our orders. Every time, the same thing happened: it seemed she couldn't even look at Grace, let alone hear her.

"Tell her what you want," I'd urge Grace. "I don't think she can hear you." Grace would run her tongue across her lips and try again. The woman always looked to me to confirm what Grace had said. *What's your problem?* I thought. *Can't you see that she's just someone who wants a grande caramel frappuccino with extra whipped cream?* But it was clear the woman couldn't see that. And this scenario repeated itself often enough that I began to conjure up possible explanations. She thought Grace was subhuman. Or that Grace shouldn't exist at all.

JEAN VANIER, IN *Becoming Human,* tells the story of Lazarus, a beggar who lived on the street in front of a wealthy man's house. Lazarus's pleas for help were ignored by the rich man, the few crumbs that fell from his table eaten by dogs. Dying within days of each other, the beggar ascended to heaven while the rich man sunk down into hell. Looking up, the rich man cried out: "Father Abraham, please send Lazarus down to put some water on my lips for I am in pain!" Abraham replied that was impossible, for between him and Lazarus was "an abyss no one can cross."

"What is this abyss that separates people?" Vanier asks. "Why are we unable to look Lazarus straight in the eye and listen to him?"

We exclude Lazarus, Vanier writes, "because we are frightened of those who are different. We are frightened of failure and rejection ... Fear is at the root of all forms of exclusion."

If we listen to Lazarus, Vanier says, we might be moved by his story. We might want to help him, and if we do that, he writes, "we risk our lives being changed."

THAT THERE WAS an abyss between the Asian woman and Grace was clear. But the truth was I didn't know what was behind her apparent aversion to Grace. And I recognized myself in her. How often had I averted my face, uneasy, even disturbed by someone who fell outside the norm? At those times I thought I understood how she felt. I wanted to lean across the counter, to catch her eye, and say, *There's something I need to tell you.*

ONE DAY I receive a new e-mail from Grace: *Bonjour, bonsoir Judy! For the Friday afternoon at Starbucks at two thirty, that would be great.*

Friday afternoon. I find a table by the window, and as I'm hanging my jacket over a chair, Grace and Jessica arrive. Jessica's face breaks into her wide smile as she bobs in a small bow. Behind her mother, Grace looks up at me. Her face puffy, big pouches under her eyes. She has a new haircut, a blunt cut just below her ears, with a straight part on one side, her bangs clipped back by a bobby pin. She wraps her arms tightly around me, pushing her head into my shoulder. After a moment, I loosen my hug, but she doesn't let go.

"Hey, Grace," I say, "what's up?"

She pushes her head harder against me and tightens her hold. After a moment, I ease away and finally, she lets go.

"I really, really miss you," she says.

My birthday, the reason for our get-together, has just passed. As Jessica returns with our coffees, Grace settles into the chair beside me. "How old are you now, Grace?" I ask.

Her face darkens. "Twenty-nine." It's been five years, I realize, since Grace and I first met. She bends her head and pulls her cellphone out of her bag, suddenly intent on texting.

As I try to figure out why Grace seems unhappy, Jessica talks to me in a low voice. "Right now, things are very difficult. This morning, she yells at David and me. She always wants to watch the YouTube. *Sailor Moon,* the TV show she likes. It has real actors, not animated, and I don't like the attitude. So I tell her she can only watch some, not all day."

Grace looks up. "She always tells me, stop watching! But I like the YouTube. Jeez."

It's a clash I've seen before. Jessica, from a culture where parents expect to be obeyed, knocking heads with Grace, who's grown up in a culture where disobedience is almost a rite of passage.

"Are you still volunteering?" I ask.

Grace nods. "I deliver the mail. To the seniors." She fills in the details. "I push the cart with the mail and knock on the doors. If someone answers, I give them their mail. And sometimes I put it under their door. One old man is mean! Sometimes he yells."

"Do you go by yourself when you deliver the mail?"

"No. My friend takes the chocolate cart. We sell chocolate!"

Jessica adds, "And an aide goes with them all the time."

Over the years I've known her, Grace has worked at several volunteer jobs. They have all been unpaid, but some have held out the promise of paid employment "if things work out." None have worked out. Sometimes the funding that supports Grace for an initial period of training runs out or is cut off. Recently, Grace worked for six months with a company that promised to pay but never did.

Grace's experience is not unusual. The unemployment rate in Canada for people with intellectual disabilities is almost 70 percent. Of those who do find employment, almost half have incomes that fall below the poverty level.

As we finish our coffees, I offer to drive Grace home so Jessica can do some shopping on her own. Jessica nods, her wide smile reappearing as she picks up her bag. She gives me a hurried bow before she turns to leave. Her step seems lighter, faster than when she came into the coffee shop. I realize how rare this kind of break is for her, as small as it is. Once her mother has left, Grace's face drops again.

"What is it?" I ask.

Grace looks down at the table as she tells me she had a fight with her boyfriend. The story comes out haltingly. "I failed his mission," Grace tells me, several times. As I try to piece together what happened, I worry that she's encountered what many young women encounter, a boyfriend who can be thoughtless, even cruel. She tells me that her mother wants her to forget him. "We've gone out for three years," Grace says, looking up at me. "I love him deeply. More than anyone else in the world. I don't want to forget him."

It's not a fairy-tale ending for Grace. Her prince is human after all, as she is. And I suspect that Grace, like many of us, is in love with the idea of romantic love. That what she's hanging onto is not the real Ronald, but the fictional one she's created, the prince who called down to her from the helicopter as she stood on the deck of the *Titanic*: *Don't be afraid. Just look up into my eyes. I think you can do it.*

I think of what I might say to Kathleen, or one of our boys, in similar circumstances. That this will pass and you'll find someone else. A better someone. But I know for Grace, this possibility is far less likely than it is for my children. That her world is a much smaller one where the possibilities for a relationship are limited to a very small subset of those who like her, are the high-functioning intellectually challenged.

As we finish our coffees, Grace slides a gift-wrapped package across the table. I pull the paper off and find a T-shirt, just my size, with a mixture of French and English across the front—*mais tu es belle*, followed mysteriously by *a cloud lets go of*.

"I love it!" I say. "Thank you, Grace."

NOT LONG AFTER my meeting with Grace, Kathleen called me late one night. I rolled over, groggily reaching for my cellphone. "Mum." My daughter's voice, as compelling as it was when she was a small girl. "Mum. You remember—?" She named the director of her theatre program, a man she'd grown to greatly admire, someone she feared would die of AIDS before she graduated. "Well, he came into our class today and talked. For two hours. It was so great."

Still groggy, I waited for her to continue, but the silence stretched out. "What did he say?"

"He said 'It's a big life. It may not be long, but it's big.'" Another pause. "Isn't that great?"

I couldn't say anything. Instantly, I was taken back to that early morning following my graduation from high school, the night when seven young people, including several from my class, died in a car accident. How in that moment, it felt like the universe was smacking us down, telling us that the world was not shimmering with possibilities, as we'd thought only the night before, but was a small, mean, and cold place. And how I'd let that feeling hold me back and stop me from opening doors until many years later.

"Mum." Kathleen sensed that I'd drifted away from her. "What's going on?"

I wanted to say something about how these words were an astounding gift, one that she could hang onto in those moments when they seemed like a cruel lie. How it took me a long time to find my way to something like them on my own.

In the dark, Jim asleep beside me, Kathleen on the other end of the line, I struggled to find a way to tell Kathleen what I thought about what she'd just said. "Those words, Kath? Don't forget them. They—" I paused. "They can save you."

IN HIS INTRODUCTION to *Becoming Human*, Jean Vanier writes:

> Is it not the life undertaking of all of us... to become human? It can be a long and sometimes painful process. It involves a growth to freedom, an opening up of our hearts to others, no longer hiding behind masks or behind the walls of fear or prejudice. It means discovering our common humanity.

PART SIX

A Big News

ONE DAY NOT long after our meeting at Starbucks, Jessica sends me a brief e-mail: *Dear Judy, Share the good news. Jessica.*

Attached to the e-mail is an article from the local newspaper: "Grace's Hard Work Pays Off." The article describes how Grace, with the assistance of an employment agency that specializes in helping those with mental disabilities, first found a temporary job at a party supply store, then, building on the success she had there, landed a permanent job at a fabric store. Grace's job is to organize the notions section and help with restocking. A photo shows Grace at the party supply store, wearing a black T-shirt that proclaims *boo*. "I like putting the threads away and helping the customers," Grace is quoted as saying.

A few weeks later, Grace and I attend a lecture about the *Titanic* offered by one of our local universities. As we settle into our seats, Grace pulls something out of her bag and holds it up to me, a wide grin splitting her face. I realize it's a paycheque from the fabric store. "Fantastic, Grace," I say.

Grace carefully slides the cheque back in her wallet. "I just wanted to surprise you."

THE SUBJECT LINE of the latest e-mail from Grace is impossible to ignore: *A Big News!*

I really want you to be at The Ground Breaking for Housing For Young Adult With Disability Place; because I am going to be in! In The Future. Here is Date: Friday January 18 at 1:00 o'clock! See You Soon. Grace

For several years, Jessica has told me about HYAD, or Housing for Young Adults with Disabilities, a non-profit society that a group of parents formed to provide assisted housing for their adult children, who, like Grace, all have some mental disability. The parents, not satisfied with the current government model that promotes house-sharing for adults with disabilities—they are mostly basement suites, Jessica told me one day, *very lonely*—decided to try a new approach. Each of the fourteen families would contribute forty thousand dollars, and with support from local and provincial governments, they would build safe, affordable housing for their children and others to follow.

The North Vancouver School District, disposing of a surplus school property, agreed to donate part of the land to HYAD. A developer came on board. But there was no money in the BC Housing budget for the project. In the financial crisis of 2008, the developer pulled out. The families were told that if they wanted to go ahead, they would have to raise the funds themselves. It seemed as if the project was about to fail. Jessica said, "Some families even cry." But they carried on. A new developer took over, and after a provincial election, money was found for the project. The city also waived some taxes.

For parents like Jessica and David, worry about their mentally challenged child can loom large as they grow old. Where will my adult child live? Who will look after her? And often there's a reluctance to ask a sibling to take on all the responsibility.

The day of the groundbreaking is a cold clear day in mid-January. A white canopy has been set up over a gravel pad. Under the canopy are a lectern and several rows of fold-up chairs and, behind the lectern, a trio of flags. A small crowd begins to gather. Most of them, I realize, know each other.

In a few minutes, I spot Grace and her parents. Grace gives me one of her fierce hugs, saying, "I really, really wanted you to be here."

A few short speeches. The mayor of North Vancouver, along with the provincial member of the legislature, confirms that the province will kick in 5.3 million dollars toward the project, and a young man, one of the intended residents, beams as he says, *I'm excited to have a chance to live here. Thank you.* And representing the parents who've fought so long for this moment is the doctor who delivered our children, the one I was sure would have suggested I have an abortion if Down syndrome or any other serious disability had been detected. Someone I haven't seen for over twenty years. Her daughter, a dark-haired young woman, one of the intended residents, sits beside her mother and claps enthusiastically.

As the groundbreaking ceremony ends, I introduce myself to the doctor who delivered our children. She stares at me as if she's trying to retrieve me from what must have been hundreds of patients whose babies she delivered. After a moment, she laughs. "So you're the writer who worked with Grace," she says. I nod and we agree to meet.

A few days later we meet for coffee and I ask her the question I've wanted to ask since I began researching this book. "Would you have suggested an abortion if my amniocentesis had indicated Down syndrome?"

She shakes her head. "No. I never would have counselled that. Never."

● ● ●

THE SUMMER AFTER graduation from her university drama program, Kathleen found a position as an intern at a theatre production company. Although at first it she called it "Plan B"—in other words, not following her original dream to act—she soon grew to love what she was doing. "Even though it's business," she told me, "everyone has some kind of creative background. They're kind of like me."

The following September, she began a master's program that focused on business and the performing arts. "I want to work behind the scenes," she told me one night in a phone call. "Maybe try to produce something some day." I heard an ease in her voice, as if she had decided, or accepted, something about herself.

"That's a great idea," I said. "Who knows how it will go."

Kathleen laughed. "Oh, Mum," she said, "you never give up hope."

• • •

BUT WITH GRACE and her play, I knew something had to change. Once I realized how difficult it would be for either of us to turn her book into a play, I encouraged her to try writing some poems.

"What about?" she asked.

"Anything, a poem can be about anything you like."

In a few days, Grace sent me a poem about taking the bus to her volunteer job. Another one about a friend who cried at the bus stop. And then she sent me this:

My Real Truth
I don't know how to describe me as a real person
Sometimes I can't even control my hot anger
Like a volcano's magma fire anger

There is something more about my dad's father—
he calls me a Down syndrome He tries to
persuade my dad, David, to send me away in a
leaving institute
For me it's okay to have Down syndrome but for the
    other people
I hate them to say that
My real truth is that I am smart and the whole world
    doesn't know and believe in me.

As I read Grace's poem, I was struck by the truth of her words. And I recognized that not so long ago, I was part of "the whole world," someone who didn't know and believe in Grace. Someone who, as a young girl, was afraid that the doughnut girl in my hometown would cast a dark spell over me. That somehow she would force me to look at myself, really look, and I wouldn't like what I saw. That I might even see some of her in me. And as loath as I am to admit this now, it may also have been something else altogether—that I feared that in the doughnut girl's presence, I could become as sadistic as Charlene and Marlene in Alice Munro's story. That something vicious lurked just beneath my surface.

● ● ●

THERE ARE ONLY little wisps of the doughnut girl. I don't even know her name. Or what happened to her or where she is now. But fragments of memory taunt me:

A sunny afternoon, school's over, walking along the main street. Friends beside me. We're going to one of our houses to play the game we've been playing for days now. Our dolls are small girls like us. We're the moms, sometimes wise, sometimes jaded, bored, or cranky. Like our own moms. Lately, one of our girls has become, with the help of a cloth stuffed under her outfit, very fat. And stupid. In my pink bedroom, we act out our walks home. My girl gets close to the fat stupid girl and hisses at her, "You're a dumb retard, you know that?"

I can't decide if this is a memory or if it's something I've imagined. How it might have been, if I'd been bold, if someone had dared me to say it.

In another fragment, I say nothing. My friends say the words. But I don't try to stop it. I don't speak up.

•••

THE DOUGHNUT GIRL. What became of her? What kind of life has she had? Is she happy?

As I think about her, a small movie begins to play in my head, one where a nameless dark-haired woman plays my role.

Walking along the main street, the dark-haired woman is struck by how much it feels the same as when she lived here. How she seems to be passing people she once knew. How they nod at her, as if she'd never left, and she nods back, reverting to the small-town code that dictates that everyone must be greeted, no matter what. How some of those who nod give off a whiff of defeat, of having long ago succumbed to the smallness of this place. Even now, almost three decades later, she can feel the same urge she'd felt as a teenager to grab those passersby, give them a hard shake, tell them that they could stay here, stuck in Nowheresville, but she was leaving. She was going to see the world. Be someone, go someplace. She almost laughs out loud now, remembering how she'd felt a burning desire to escape, combined with a sick fear that she'd end up like them, shuffling along the same street all her life.

But now she sees that almost everything about the main street has changed in the years since she left. The place where the buses idled, sending a plume of white exhaust into the early pink light, the men with their black lunch buckets waiting in a silent ragged line, the blue-and-white co-op building, have been transformed. Now it's a new liquor store, one that could be in any suburb, full of clever displays of staff picks, finds from New Zealand and Chile. Nothing like the old store she went to with her father, where a stern clerk eyed you from behind a long wooden counter, the bottles lined up on dim shelves.

On the corner by the granite steps of the bank, there's a familiar knot of boys, about thirteen or fourteen. Their voices a wash of sounds—words rising into argument, veering off into guffaws. A second of silence, followed by a shove, a shove back. Walking past them, an image floats into her mind—the slow girl, the one who used to waddle along the sidewalk with a doughnut, sometimes a fistful of doughnuts, from her parents' bakery. The one the boys called out to, like a budding chorus, *Hey, re-tard! Whatcha got there?*

In a second the dark-haired woman is seven again, feeling the same horror and fascination she'd felt when she trailed along behind the doughnut girl, listening to the taunts of the boys. As if she were glimpsing something dark and slippery that would vanish the instant an adult appeared.

The bakery has been closed for at least a decade. She'd heard that the couple who'd run it all those years had both died. What happened to their doughnut-loving daughter? Had she been forced to move to one of the group homes that had replaced, in a hit-and-miss way, the old institutions?

She walks past the old liquor store, now a real estate office specializing in condominiums at the ski hill. And there, next to it, is the bakery. Alive again. The gold-lettered words on the window the same—Thompson's Bakery, Fresh Every Day—but inside, she sees, everything is different. A new glass case with a rounded front, a gleaming wood counter. Behind it, a young man wearing a red paisley bandana smiles at her as she steps inside. *Good morning,* he says, *what can I get for you?* Like the many other young people who've moved into the town since she left, his smile is open, friendly, completely lacking in the studied indifference she's grown accustomed to in the city.

She smiles back. *Everything looks so good,* she says. Plump scones nestle beside dark cinnamon pinwheels, abutting a tray of fruit and nut-dotted muffins. On the wall behind the counter, rows of bread and buns, the same choices she'd have at home in the city, whole wheat, gluten-free, even chia-seed enhanced.

The old bakery, the one the dark-haired woman remembers, was nothing like this. Flour-dusted, it specialized in square white sandwich loaves, glazed doughnuts, white hot dog buns that she and her brothers would tear apart and roll into tiny balls for dough wars.

The family who used to own this bakery, she asks the young man. *Did you ever meet any of them?*

You mean the Thompsons?

The dark-haired woman nods. *And they had a daughter, I can't remember her—*

You must mean Jeanette. The young man turns and waves at someone in the back. The dark-haired woman stares as a heavy middle-aged woman wearing an apron emerges from the back.

Jeanette, he says, *this is someone who remembers your mom and dad.*

Jeanette's hair, pulled back tight, is beginning to grey, her cheeks still fat puffs that almost hide her eyes. She swipes a floury hand along the side of her apron. Hi, she says. Hi.

Jeanette's eyes are a soft blue-grey.

The dark-haired woman leans across the counter, holds out her hand and smiles. *Hi, Jeanette. How are you?*

Jeanette smiles at her. *I'm good,* she says.

I NEVER MET Jeanette. I don't know if that's her name. I don't know what happened to her. But I am the dark-haired woman.

• • •

AT THE END of her book, Grace describes how she reunites with her mother, who turned into a white angel bird when she died. As Cinderella-Grace and Prince Ronald ride in a helicopter, the white angel bird appears alongside, and when the door opens, *She flies in like a dark Titanic blue wave and transforms into an elegant human lady, wearing a dark Titanic blue gown, the same colour that I wore to the royal grand ball!* Cinderella-Grace fills her mother in on what's happened since she died—her father remarrying; being treated like a "castle maid"; Prince Ronald falling in love and marrying her, having three baby girls; and she and her prince training to become "really important" international spies, which *can be a really dangerous past-time and it makes us work alone a lot!*

My mother smiles at me, Grace writes, *and says she is glad that I am happy.* And then Grace describes the place she and her prince have found in the world:

After several years as international spies, Prince Ronald and I become known far and wide. Prince Ronald becomes the royal grand golden crown king, and I become the royal grand golden crown Queen, and we live in our royal grand golden castle with our three beautiful daughters, who are doing well in their training to become spies.

• • •

ONE FRIDAY WHEN Grace was in her room looking for something she wanted to show me, Jessica and I started talking about names.

"How did you choose names for your children?" she asked. "Was it hard to agree?"

I laughed and shook my head. "I named our boys after my brothers and Kathleen after my mother. Jim didn't have any real say in it, but, luckily, he liked those names." I paused. "Growing up, I worshipped my older brother John, and David, three years younger than me, was someone I always wanted to protect. And my mother..." I stopped for a moment. "I wanted her to live forever."

"For me," Jessica said, "I think what names can help each of them. Albert, I name after Albert Einstein, because I hope he will be brilliant."

"And Grace?"

Jessica smiled. "I chose Grace because I hope her name will help everyone accept her."

• • •

AS GRACE AND I were nearing the end of working on her book, I asked her one day what her dreams were. I'm not sure why I asked her, but maybe it's as simple as that by then

I realized Grace would have dreams like everyone else.

"My dreams?" Grace hesitated, as if she'd never been asked about her dreams.

"What things do you dream about for yourself, for your life?"

Grace pushed her finger across the plastic covering her dining room table, tracing some invisible pattern. As the moment stretched out, she looked down at the table, just as she had that first day we met, and then she whispered, her voice so low I had to bend close to hear her, "My impossible dream is to find somebody to love."

■ ■ ■

THERE'S SOMETHING I *need to tell you.* I'm not sure I can find the words, but it goes something like this. This young woman standing in front of you, the one who's running her thick tongue across her lips, the one you can't look at? Once I was like you. I didn't want to look at her. I was afraid of her, afraid of what she might reveal about myself. But now, what can I tell you now? She knows English and Mandarin and she wants to learn French. She loves Starbucks. She's written a book and she has a paying job. She has dreams. She knows how you feel. She's like you and she's like me. She's one of us.

REFERENCES

Bales v. Central Okanagan School District 23, (1984), 54 B.C. Law Reports 203.

Beck, Martha. 1999. *Expecting Adam.* New York: Berkley Books.

Bérubé, Michael. 1996. *Life As We Know It.* New York: Vintage Books.

Black, Edwin. 2003. *War against the Weak.* New York: Four Walls Eight Windows.

Buck v. Bell, 27 U.S. 200.

Chen, Grace. 2006. *Cinderella-Grace, Vancouver Princess.* Vancouver: Self-published.

Churchill, Winston. "Care of the Mentally Retarded, July 15, 1910." In *Blood, Toil, Tears and Sweat: Speeches of Winston Churchill* (Boston, 1989). Quoted in Wright, *Downs,* p. 84.

Curtis, Wayne. 2006. "Breaking the Ice." *Canadian Geographic,* March–April.

Dix, Dorothea. "Memorial to the Massachusetts Legislature, 1843." Quoted in Wright, *Downs,* p. 43.

Dugdale, Richard L. 1877. *The Jukes: A Study in Crime, Pauperism, Disease and Heredity.* New York: Putnam.

E. (Mrs.) v. Eve, [1986] 2 S.C.R. 388.

Goddard, Henry. 1912. *The Kallikak Family: A Study in the Heredity of Feeble-Mindedness.* New York: Macmillan.

"Grace's Hard Work Pays Off," *North Shore News,* 2012, p.27.

Hurley, Dan. 2011. "All I Could Think Is, She's My Baby, She's a Lovely Girl and What Can I Do to Help Her?" *New York Times Magazine,* July 31, 28.

Kingsley, Emily Perl. 1987. "Welcome to Holland." All rights reserved. Reprinted by permission of the author.

Langdon Down, John. 2009. "The Education and Training of the Feeble in Mind." In O. Conor Ward, *Dr. John Langdon Down and Normansfield,* 2nd Revised edition (July 2009). Teddington, Sussex: The Langdon Down Centre Trust.

Langdon Down, John. 1867. "Observations on an Ethnic Classification of Idiots." *Journal of Mental Science 13.* Quoted in Wright, *Downs,* p. 194.

Laughlin, Harry Hamilton. 1922. "Eugenical Sterilization in the United States." Psychopathic Laboratory of the Municipal Court of Chicago, December.

Makin, Kirk. 2012. "School Discriminated against Boy by Cutting Special-Needs Program: Top Court." *Globe and Mail,* November 9.

McMartin, Pete. 2008. "Soccer Team a Dream Come True for Special Needs Children." *Vancouver Sun,* April 5.

Moore v. British Columbia (Education), 2012 SCC 61.

Munro, Alice. 2009. *Too Much Happiness.* Toronto: McClelland and Stewart.

Murphy, Robert. 1990. *The Body Silent.* London: W.W. Norton.

Rice, Lynette. 2012. "Actors with Down Syndrome." *Entertainment Weekly,* March 2, accessed December 20, 2013, http://www.ew.com/ew/inside/ issue/0,ewTax:1196,00.html.

Sample, Ian. 2013. "Down's Syndrome Cells 'Fixed' in First Step Towards Chromosome Therapy." *The Guardian,* July 17.

Society of Obstetricians and Gynaecologists of Canada. 2007. "Prenatal Screening for Fetal Aneuploidy," SOGC Clinical Practice Guideline No. 187, February, accessed December 22, 2013, http://www.jogc.com/abstracts/ full/200702_SOGCClinicalPracticeGuidelines_1.pdf.

Solomon, Andrew. 2012. *Far from the Tree.* New York: Simon and Schuster.

Vanier, Jean. 1998. *Becoming Human.* Toronto: House of Anansi Press.

Ward, Bruce. 2008. "Airbrushing Away Diversity." *The Ottawa Citizen,* March 2.

Wright, David. 2011. *Downs: The History of a Disability.* Oxford: Oxford University Press.

ACKNOWLEDGEMENTS

MANY PEOPLE ENCOURAGED me to write this book and generously shared their stories with me. To all of them, I am profoundly grateful.

Madelyne Mackenzie set this book in motion when she introduced me to Grace. West Vancouver United Church hosted Grace's book launch. Early on, Yvonne Gall of the Canadian Broadcasting Corporation helped me produce a short radio documentary about Grace. Fiona Lam, Susan Olding, Rachel Rose, and Jane Silcott urged me to turn the essay I kept trying to write into a book. Judy Morrison, Joan Lee, and Judy Gandossi read drafts and gave me feedback.

While working with Joan Thomas of the Banff Wired Writing program, I saw, for the first time, that this could be a book. Claudia Casper of Betsy Warland's Vancouver Manuscript Intensive program inspired me to write a bigger book than what I'd written so far. The moment when Carolyn Forde, my agent, e-mailed to say she'd like to read my entire manuscript was a high point in this journey. Anna Comfort O'Keeffe and the team at Harbour Publishing and Douglas & McIntyre have worked very hard to make this happen. Maureen Nicholson gave me careful and thoughtful editorial feedback. Denise Chong of the Sage Hill Writing program helped me find a clearer structure and put her finger on a vital missing section of my manuscript.

To Russell Morfitt, his parents Peggy and George, Scott Jones and his mother Janet, Cindy Burdett, Susan Anthony and her mother Lorna, to Dale Froese and Laurel Griffin, thank you for sharing your stories.

My wonderful writing group, the Lying Bastards—Sally Breen, Dina Del Bucchia, Keri Korteling, Nancy Lee, Denise Ryan, Carol Shaben and John Vigna—listened to me read sections of my book, sometimes over and over, and gave me invaluable feedback. When I thought I was getting nowhere, more than once, they refused to let me give up.

Without Jessica and David Chen's trust and openness, this book would not exist. To them, I owe enormous appreciation.

Grace has changed how I see the world. She has opened my heart in a way I once would have thought impossible. Thank you beyond thank you, Grace.

Finally, to my family—my parents, who taught me to dream, my sons David and John, who unfailingly encouraged me, my daughter Kathleen, who let me share her dreams, and my husband Jim, who said when I wanted to write, "try it, see where it takes you"—thank you, from the bottom of my heart.

—J.K.M., VANCOUVER, BC, JANUARY 2014

**For information on purchasing a copy of Grace's book, please go to
www.douglas-mcintyre.com/book/cinderella-grace**